June 26, 1996     9 סיון 5756

Dear Mrs. Goldstein,

We would like to thank you for all the energy and year of teaching you provided for Kyle in Grade 2 this year. We all wish you and your family continued good health, happiness and prosperity.     Fondly,

Henry, Hyla, Kyle Danya & Haley Borenstein

# The Expulsion of the Jews

# THE EXPULSION OF THE JEWS

## Five Hundred Years of Exodus

YALE STROM

S.P.I. BOOKS
New York

S.P.I. BOOKS

A division of Shapolsky Publishers, Inc.

Copyright © 1992 by Yale Strom

For any additional information, contact:
S.P.I. Books/Shapolsky Publishers, Inc.
136 West 22nd Street
New York, NY 10011
(212) 633-2022 / FAX (212) 633-2123

10 9 8 7 6 5 4 3 2 1

ISBN: 1-56171-082-2

Library of Congress Cataloging-in-Publication Data

Layout design by Yale Strom
Typography by Smith, Inc., New York

Manufactured in the United States of America

FRONT COVER PHOTOS
Right front: Sofia, Bulgaria—Cantor Khaim Meshulam; Lower left:
Split, Yugoslavia—Passageway to former Jewish Quarter; Top: Izmir,
Turkey—Looking for the *Torah* passage for the *Fast of Tevet.*
BACK COVER PHOTO
Sevilla, Spain—Former Jewish Quarter, the "Juderia."

*Dedicated to:*
*The Sephardim of the Expulsion,*
*their descendants, Jewish and Converso.*

# TABLE OF CONTENTS

# ACKNOWLEDGMENTS

I WOULD LIKE TO THANK the following people who helped make this book possible by providing me with invaluable help and hospitality and helping me with the research in their communities:

Marina Lasić and Ivan Čerešnješ of Sarajevo; Eduard Tauber of Split; Marina Deleon and Mr. Conkič of Belgrade (Head administrators of the Jewish camp in Pirovac); Benjamin Samokovlija and Žaklina Risteska of Skopje; Josef Levi and Clara Armandova of Sofia; Rabbi Isak Haleva and Karen Gerson of Istanbul; Binyamin Avramento and Joseph Özel of Izmir; Rabbi Moche Itshak Halegua, Rena Molho and the Yiehaskiel family of Thessaloniki; Iacov Filoys of Larissa; Ilias Kones of Volos; Israel and Esther Kapeta of Trikala; Mrs. Lydia Eshkenazi and Mr. Abraham Minos Sassoon of Athens; Mario and Esther Maissis of Khalkis; Dino and Karin Delmonte; Adam and Laila Delmonte, Rabbi Moshe Bendahan; Rabbi Garson, Veronica Nehama Masri and Berta Sarria of Madrid; Simon Hassan Benasayag of Sevilla; Rabbi Abraham Assor, David Ruah, Miriam Assor, João Guerra, Henrique Ettner and Raphael Bensadon of Lisbon. Special thanks to J's Lab in Oak Park, Michigan, for its careful work in printing the photographs.

The following were invaluable for their assistance in translating the interviews: Suzanna, Spiro and Vasilios Eleftheriades and Bella and Nissim Alhades.

I want to thank the American Jewish Joint Distribution Committee, Inc. for their support and interest, not only in my work, but in the work and financial assistance they provide for hundreds of Jewish communities throughout the world.

I express extreme gratitude to my agent, Mary Jack Wald, and my friend and traveling companion in Turkey and Thessaloniki, Alan Alhades, who adroitly translated my informants' Judeo-Spanish into English.

Most of all, I would like to thank my wife Joasia, whose ancestral lineage on her mother's side is Sephardic originally from Córdoba. Her keen eye, in editing the thousands of photographs and patience with my occasional kvetching hewed a precise course for the completion of this book.

# INTRODUCTION

*I*n March of 1492, King Ferdinand and Queen Isabella, having reconquered the last remnants of the Moslem empire, signed an Edict of Expulsion, requiring Spain's 200,000 Jews to either convert to Christianity or leave the country. By boat and by foot they left, all required to pay an exit fee for the right to do so.

*The Expulsion of the Jews* is a portrait of the Jews who—in 1992—will commemorate the expulsion of ancestors who trace their lineage to the Middle Ages, when their descendants lived in the Iberian Peninsula—Jews who, according to stories passed down through the five hundred years, left Spain marching, singing religious songs, led by their rabbis. They were called Sephardim.

The name Sephardim had its origins from a specific exegesis of the prophet Obadiah, in whose writings Sephard meant an unidentified country to which Jews were exiled from Jerusalem. In the Medieval Ages, Jewish scholars were positive that Sepharad was the ancient name of Spain and Portugal. Consequently, following the expulsion of the Jews from Spain in 1492, and from Portugal in 1496, the Jews from the Iberian Peninsula and their descendants—were called Sephardim.

The expulsion sent 200,000 Sephardim along perilous paths to uncertain futures. They formed a new diaspora, a dispersion within a dispersion. Not only did they long to be in the land of Israel someday, but, because of their long sojourn in Spain, they wished to continue their Sephardic culture. Their determination to retain their Jewish tongue, Judeo-Spanish (the Jewish vernacular consisting mainly of Castellan, Turkish, Arabic, Greek and Hebrew words and idioms), along with their strong-willed Sephardic consciousness of Sephardic culture, soon assimilated other Jews living along the Aegean coast and in the Balkans. After their expulsion, the bulk of the exiles

found refuge in the vast and powerful Ottoman Empire. By the 1930s, some eighty three percent living in the region, numbering 200,000, were still Sephardim.

But the Holocaust, relocation to Israel and the natural attrition due to old age has caused this number to dwindle to 50,000.

In *The Expulsion of the Jews*, through historical description, personal narrative and pictorial representation, you will become acquainted with the Sephardim who still live in the countries in which their ancestors sought refuge five hundred years ago. Some of these kehillot (Hebrew: Jewish communities) are stable, but most are diminishing. The oldest and largest can be found in Bulgaria, Greece, Turkey and Yugoslavia.

The photographs and text also comprise a commemorative to those Jews who chose to return to Spain and Portugal. (In Portugal, there are some Jews today who trace their ancestry to the time of the expulsion and earlier and never left the country.)

Having researched extensively the history and culture of Jews living in Eastern Europe today, I felt confident my field research among the Sephardic kehillot would go smoothly. This was not to be.

During the initial stages of my travels, I often felt I was a stranger in a strange land. The physical landscapes of the countries were quite different, with many of the kehillot close to or on the sea, as opposed to the many land-locked kehillot I visited in Eastern Europe. The beautiful architecture of their homes and synagogues reflected the strong cultural influences of the Turks and Muslims. The cuisine was different. Older Jews spoke Judeo-Spanish and their singing of Ladino romancero (folk ballads) reflected this difference. Even their manner of synagogue worship and liturgical melodies was a new experience for me.

But, occasionally, the greatest obstacle was the reserved ethnic pride which sometimes caused the people to be uncooperative. This highborn attitude was perhaps internalized under the influence of the Spanish *grandeza* (nobility). Spaniards tended to put an extreme value on their *limpieza ale sangre* (cleanliness of blood), which often translated itself into an air of being "un-haimish."

This quality was clearly demonstrated to me by the fact that, in over three months of traveling, only twice was I invited for an erev Shabbat meal. In Eastern Europe it was a rare erev Shabbat when I was not sharing a meal with a Jewish family from the kehille.

However, after trekking thousands of miles from Istanbul to Lisbon, meeting hundreds of Jews and taking 5,000 photographs, I began to understand the difficulties these Sephardim had in maintaining their culture. (This research was done during the Persian Gulf War, which height-

ened the suspicion and made my informants more security conscious.) I did make many new friends and learned to understand the Sephardim tenacity for order within their kehille and respect for family pedigree (yikhus). Perhaps it has been these attributes that have kept the Sephardim religiously and culturally whole for half a millennium.

The Sephardim lived for more than one thousand years on the Iberian peninsula and created one of the greatest epochs in Jewish history—the Golden Age of Spain. Then, suddenly and mercilessly, Jewish culture came to a virtual end as the Catholic Church forced Jews to convert to Christianity or be murdered. Eventually, those remaining were expelled from their homeland.

The words and images in these pages are not only a commemoration of the 500th anniversary of the Jews' expulsion from Spain and Portugal. They are also a celebration of their survival and continuance in the Balkans.

Larissa: Jewish Day School students.

# *Yugoslavia*

Before Slovenia and Croatia declared their independence from war-torn Yugoslavia, Jews lived in all six republics and two provinces that made up the country. Each was unique because of its specific history and culture. Prior to the founding of Yugoslavia, following the end of World War I in 1918, each of the republics and provinces—Slovenia, Croatia, Serbia, Bosnia-Hercegovina, Montenegro, Macedonia, Vojvodina and Kosovo—had a Jewish history of its own.

Of all the Balkan countries, Yugoslavia is the only one with a sizable Ashkenazic community as well as Sephardic. Generally, the Jews of Slovenia and Croatia trace their lineage to those of Central Europe, while the Jews in the republics of central and southern Yugoslavia trace their immediate ancestry to Jews from Greece and Turkey, whose ancestors originally came from the Iberian peninsula.

Jews first settled in Yugoslavia during Roman times, as evidenced by synagogue and tombstone inscriptions found near Split (Spalato), on the Dalmatian coast. These excavations date from the third century C.E. Small Ashkenazic communities existed in Serbia and Croatia in the Middle Ages. Following the expulsion in 1492, Sephardic Jews started migrating to the Dalmatian coast from Spain, Portugal and Italy by way of Thessaloniki. By 1521, this area of Yugoslavia was under Turkish rule, and the Jewish communities came under the authority of the Haham Bashi, the chief Rabbi of Constantinople.

Life for the Sephardim under Turkish rule was manageable, but it was not until the Treaty of Berlin, in 1878, that Jews were granted complete civil, economic and political emancipation in Serbia. The Jews in the other regions did not become full legal citizens until the end of World War I, when the modern country of Yugoslavia was established.

With an influx of Jews from the former Austro-Hungarian territories, Yugoslavia's Jewish population swelled to 76,654 in 1931. The Sephardim comprised about 30,000 and the Ashkenazim about 46,000, of which some 22,000 were Hungarian. The Sephardim were organized into thirty-seven religious communities. The wealthier Sephardic communities were in Serbia and Croatia, while those in the other republics were poorer. Prior to the war, the largest Sephardic community was in Sarajevo. Nearly eighty percent of the 13,000 Jews were Sephardic. Until the 1930s, anti-Semitism had not been a part of Jewish life, but, gradually, it began to seep in from Germany. The Croatians and Volksdeutsche were the most eager to accept this virulent and anti-Semitic propaganda and became overwhelmingly pro-German. With a number of Jewish refugees fleeing Central Europe to Yugoslavia, the government felt compelled to initiate its first two anti-Jewish laws in October of 1940. The first limited the access of Jews to high schools and higher education, the second stopped granting Jews licenses for opening new businesses and restricted the renewal of those licenses already granted.

On April 6, 1941, German forces, along with their Italian, Bulgarian and Hungarian allies, invaded Yugoslavia. Eleven days later, the Yugoslavian government capitulated to the Nazis, though the partisan forces in the forests and mountains continued their resistance until the end of the war. Some 5,000 Jews were prominent in the partisans. The medical staff was almost entirely Jewish and the second-in-command—after Marshall Tito—was a Jew, Moises Pijade. After the war, Moises Pijade became Vice President, then President, of the Yugoslav Federal Parliament. By the end of 1941, Belgrade became the first capital city in occupied Europe which was completely "Judenrein." Those few Jews that were able to escape were hunted down by Serbian collaborators. Some 60,000 Yugoslavian Jews perished in the Holocaust, many in the infamous concentration camps located in Nĭs (Macedonia), Šabac (Serbia), and the largest Jasenovac (Croatia). After the war, between the years 1948 and 1951, about 9,000 Jews immigrated to Israel.

Today, there are only 6,000 Jews in the country. Of these, thirty percent are of Sephardic origin. Sephardim are living throughout the country, though large numbers are still found in the cities that once had a thriving Sephardic culture. No distinct Sephardic communities remain because of the high rate of assimilation and intermarriage with the Ashkenazim and gentile population.

Religious life was never very strong in Yugoslavia. Twelve synagogues are open for worship during the High Holidays, less for other holidays and only two for regular Shabbat services. These are in Zagreb and Belgrade. Of the twelve, only the ones in Dubrovnik and Split are Sephardic in origin.

Secular culture activities do exist with a full range, including two Jewish kindergartens, communal Seders, Jewish choirs, museums, community clubs, a Maccabiah sports festival every year, Jewish lectures, libraries, symposiums, Hebrew and history classes and a Jewish camp at Pirovac.

The recent rise of anti-Semitism in the former Eastern Bloc countries has become a concern for the Jews in Yugoslavia, particularly in Croatia. More daunting, however, are diminishment due to immigration to Israel, assimilation, intermarriage, low birth rate and the country's bloody civil war. The civil strife puts the members of the small, but visible, Jewish community in a position where they may be forced to choose between being loyal to their own republic or be accused of aiding the enemy if they try to remain as one neutral, cohesive unit.

# SARAJEVO

Sarajevo, the capital—and largest city—of the republic of Bosnia and Hercegovina, was conquered by the Turks in the early part of the fifteenth century. Sephardic refugees from Spain and Portugal then formed the first Jewish community in Sarajevo in 1565.

Generally, the Jews had good relations with their Muslim rulers and neighbors. They built their first synagogue in 1587—appropriately named in the Spanish tradition, Il Cal Grande —in the Jewish quarter known as "El Cortijo" (the communal yard). As the community grew, Jews also lived elsewhere in the city without any legal restrictions.

By 1850, the medical profession was predominately Jewish, while other Jews were artisans, merchants, blacksmiths, tailors, shoemakers, joiners, metal workers, butchers, and traders in iron, wood, textiles, furs and glass. In addition, their commercial connections reached throughout the Ottoman Empire and Italy. All this activity induced Jews to relocate to Sarajevo. Their number soon rose to 2,100.

In 1878, the Austro-Hungarian Empire annexed Bosnia. For the Jewish community this meant an influx of Ashkenazim to Sarajevo from Austria, Hungary, Moravia, Bohemia and Galicia, all eager to develop commercial enterprises and begin trading with Budapest, Vienna, Prague and Krakow.

Between the World Wars, the Sephardim enjoyed a culturally diverse life and paid tribute to their success by building the largest Sephardic synagogue in the Balkans. Constructed between 1927 and 1931, the synagogue was desecrated and plundered by the Croatian and German fascists during World War II. After the war, it was used as a theatre hall.

During these productive years, a Jewish high school and a rabbinical seminary opened in 1928.

The seminary was the only one in the Balkans, except for the one in Rhodes. Rabbi Zadeek Danon, the only rabbi in the entire country today, is a graduate of this seminary in Sarajevo. There were mutual aid societies such as La Benevolensia (founded in 1894), Melecha, Geula (which benefited artisans) and Lyra (a choir that promoted Judeo-Spanish music). There were active Zionist organizations and several Jewish weeklies that were printed between 1898–1941, including the first and only printed in Ladino, called *La Alborado*.

Altogether, there were one hundred and thirty organized Jewish communities in Bosnia before the war, totaling some 15,000 Jews. Sarajevo was the largest of these communities and had the fifth largest Sephardic population in the Balkans after Thessaloniki, Istanbul, Izmir, and Sofia. Of Sarajevo's 12,000 Jews, eighty percent were Sephardim.

In the spring of 1941, the Germans entered Sarajevo and normal life for the Jews ceased to exist. On a daily basis, they had to deal with requisitions, expropriations, executions of hostages for acts of sabotage, individual arrests and confinement to specific neighborhoods. Finally, during the months of September through November, the Germans—with the aid of the Croatian army—began the mass deportations. Children and the elderly were sent directly to the Jasenovac concentration camp. The able-bodied men were sent to Djakova, near Osijek, while women were sent to Loborgrad. Extermination took place in all these camps that were run by the country's own Ustachi troops. The leader of the Ustachi was Ante Pavelić, minister of Interior and Police in the puppet government of Croatia. The Jews who were sent to the island of Rab, off the coast of Yugoslavia, were spared the sadism of the Ustachi. They were under the direct control of the Italians and had the highest rate of survival of all Yugoslavian prisoners.

Also, some Jews managed to escape to the mountains, where many of them joined the partisans. 973 Jewish partisans from Sarajevo fought the Nazis and Ustachi troops side-by-side with their communist brethren. 340 were killed. After the Holocaust, the Jewish community struggled to recover. About half the survivors who returned (approximately 1,200) chose to immigrate to Israel in the late 1940s.

Today, thirty-six Jewish communities remain in Bosnia, some of which are located in Mostar, Zenica, Duboj, Tuzla, Banja Luka and Sarajevo. With about 1,000 Jews, Sarajevo is the cultural and spiritual center for the Jews of Bosnia, since it has the only operating synagogue and community center. In the last two years, there has been a small, but steady, revival of Jewish life in the city. The community center, where mostly retired Jews come to socialize, read, play cards and watch television, is open every morning. On Tuesday, Thursday and Saturday afternoons and evenings the youth come to socialize, participating in lectures, concerts, Hebrew and even Judeo-Spanish classes.

This heightened interest in Sephardic culture recently spawned the creation of a new club called Vidas Largas (Judeo-Spanish *long life*). Named after the parent organization in Paris, members of the club, led by the Ladino scholar, Dr. Isak Papo, meet once a week to read and write in Ladino and speak the language of their Sephardic ancestors.

A quiet man, Dr. Papo revealed a little of himself in the following conversation:

"I was born here in Sarajevo in 1912, which is to say I have seen, heard and read about too much bloodshed in my lifetime. Both my parents and my twelve brothers and sisters spoke Judeo-Spanish in the home. When the war started, I was captured and sent to the island of Rab. After escaping, I joined and fought with the partisans

for the remainder of the war. When I returned to Sarajevo, I found only my mother and youngest sister had survived the nightmare. Altogether, I had lost eighteen members of my family and relatives. There was no reason to stay in a country where the earth was still warm from the spilled blood of our brothers and sisters. As soon as they could, my mother and sister immigrated to Israel. I could not join them because I had not received permission from the new government. Bosnia had been severely damaged and, since I was a civil engineer, the government needed my skills to build new roads and bridges.

"I think Jewish life will still exist here in Sarajevo for several generations to come. Just last Purim, we had over one hundred children here to celebrate. But, keeping Judeo-Spanish alive is another matter entirely. My wife and I spoke Croatian to our children instead of Judeo-Spanish. When I was young, my brothers and sisters and myself had a difficult time in school because our Serbo-Croatian was poor. Today, maybe there are twenty or thirty people here in Sarajevo that really speak a fluent Judeo-Spanish. Most of these people grew up before the war. I formed Vidas Largas so we could be connected with other Jewish groups in Europe who still speak and write Ladino. Perhaps we can preserve some of the treasures and traditions of this poetic language."

Despite the odds against the Jewish community surviving several generations in the twenty-first century, the president of the community, Mr. Čerešnješ, felt there was some hope:

"Because we are living under special circumstances after the war, the middle generation virtually learned nothing about Judaism. We feel we missed something and want to urgently pass on much more to our children. We are learning along with them, even religion which only recently has become more popular. It is being transmitted to our children like medicine—drop by drop."

# SPLIT

The earliest archaeological evidence of Jewish life in Yugoslavia dates from the Roman times, in the third century C.E., when the Jews lived in Dalmatia (Croatia). The evidence is a small clay urn that was unearthed near the town of Solin, about thirty kilometers outside of Split. The Jews were dispersed when Solin was destroyed by the Avaras in a battle against the Romans in 641. In the seventh century, the Jews finally regrouped on the Adriatic Coast, in the fortified Diocletian city of Split. It is the oldest, continuous Jewish community in Yugoslavia today. Over the years, because of its strategic military and commercial location, Split has had several different rulers. From the twelfth to the fifteenth centuries, Hungary, Venice, Hungary again, and Bosnia—in that order—ruled Split. Then, from 1420 to 1797, Venice governed Split again until the French, under Napoleon, liberated the city and the Jews from their ghetto. The French remained in control until 1814, when Austria took over for one hundred years. In December of 1918, just after World War I, Yugoslavia became an independent country.

In the sixteenth century, two groups of Sephardim lived in Split. The Ponentine (western) came from Spain via Italy, while the Levantine (eastern) came from Spain via the Ottoman empire. The differences between the two communities were pronounced, but, by the late eighteenth century, both groups had merged into one stable congregation.

The Jews of Split were the primary links in the chain of trade between Venice and the Ottoman lands. Subsequently, they became quite wealthy, enjoying Split's free port status and encouraging their brethren from the Ottoman countries to settle there. Grateful for the liberal governing policies of the Venetians, the Jews successfully helped to defend Split from Turkish

attack in 1657. However, this amiable relationship began to deteriorate in the eighteenth century when the high economic status of Venice began to crumble. One result of this breakdown was the insurmountable amount of anti-Jewish laws, which forced many Jews to leave Split. Some of the laws prohibited Jews from leaving the ghetto from midnight to sunrise, forced all shops in the ghetto to be closed on the Christmas holidays and forbid the employment of any Christians by Jewish businesses.

In 1873 the Jews were finally granted full emancipation under the Austrians, and, once again, were encouraged to settle in Split. Instead of a community made up of Italian-speaking Jews, the community became increasingly Croatian-speaking, with the Jews primarily coming from Bosnia and Croatia.

Prior to World War II, the community had 450 members. When the Italians occupied Split and the surrounding areas on April 6, 1941, however, the Jewish community grew considerably larger due to the influx of refugees fleeing German-occupied Austria and Czechoslovakia. In the beginning of the occupation, the tiny, crowded ghetto was able to maintain a sense of relative calm and equilibrium as the Italians were not especially harsh. The Italian army even allowed about 2,000 Jewish refugees to transit through Split to partisan-controlled islands, despite the stern rebuke from Pavelić's quisling Croatian regime. But, later in 1942, as the war turned decidedly in favor of the Allies, the false sense of calm in the ghetto was quickly shattered.

Mrs. Blanka Danon-Nuić was born and lived in the heart of the Jewish quarters in Split. She recalls the sudden change of events:

"One erev Shabbat, just after Shavuot, without any warning, the fascists came to the synagogue and began beating the men while they were praying. The women were in the balcony and were able to escape. After the beatings, the Italians took everything they could carry from inside the synagogue. They stole Jewish books, silver ritual objects, the ark cover—even the Torahs. Then they went to the streets and began throwing rocks and smashing all the windows and doors of the Jewish businesses.

"I remember it well because my cousin owned a perfume store which was completely ruined. During that whole night there was looting, burning and random beatings throughout the ghetto. What we have today in the synagogue were the objects saved by a few gentiles. Just recently, there was a three hundred year old mezuzzah found in someone's home here in the Jewish quarter that had been hidden from the Italians."

When the Italians capitulated on September 9, 1943, the Germans entered the city. Some Jews were able to escape into the partisan-held mountains or by small boats to Italy, but most were captured by the Nazis. That October the men were sent to the Sajmište concentration camp near Belgrade. All 115 men were killed in the gas buses. Five months later their wives and children were sent to Jasenovac, where they too perished.

After the war, about 100 to 120 Jews returned to Split. Through the years, the community has diminished, primarily because of immigration to Israel and assimilation, so that today there are only eighty one Jews in the community. Another twenty reside in the nearby environs and come to the city for special occasions and to celebrate the Jewish holidays.

Jewish life is rather sparse and sporadic. There is no rabbi. For some of the Jewish holidays, such as Passover, a cantorial student from Sarajevo comes to help lead the services and the seder. When someone who has requested a Jewish burial dies, Rabbi Danon from Belgrade comes to officiate. Fifteen to twenty young Jews and their parents make up the core of the active Jews. They have a Maccabi soccer team that plays against local teams, as well as other Maccabi teams in the country; attend occasional lectures on Jewish subjects and come to relax in the cool confines of the community center. These are the activities which sustain the rhythm of Jewish life in Split.

After a long overnight bus trip from Sarajevo, I arrived in Split around 6:00 a.m. It was surprising to see as many people as I did at the station that early in the morning. A woman—who looked older than her years—grabbed my arm, all the while repeating in German "zimmer zimmer, billig zimmer" (room room, cheap room). Steadfastly, she led me through the quiet streets. Ten minutes later we arrived at her home, which looked from the inside as if it were a hostel for wayward travelers like myself.

After a shower and a breakfast of scrambled eggs, potatoes and peaches from her garden, I made my way to the Jewish community center, hoping to accomplish quite a lot this day. I slowly traversed through the cool, shaded, narrow streets of the old city. After some time, the maze of smooth-worn stone passages led me to Židovski Prolaz (Jewish alley). There, I waited at the foot of the stairs thirty or so minutes. When the head of the community, Mr. Eduard Tauber, finally arrived—speaking good English—he invited me inside for my second breakfast of the day: some Turkish coffee and biscuits. The morning was spent with some interesting conversation and several refills of the Turkish coffee.

# SKOPJE

Skopje is the capital of Macedonia, the southernmost republic in Yugoslavia. There was a Jewish settlement in nearby Bitolj (Monastir) during Roman occupation. Since Skopje lies on a known trade route, historians deduce that Jews were probably there since Roman times.

The first synagogue was built in 1361 by Ashkenazic refugees from Hungary. In the fifteenth and sixteenth centuries hundreds of Jews, expelled from the Iberian peninsula, settled in Skopje, changing the Jewish community's character forever. By the seventeenth century, most of the Ashkenazim were completely assimilated to the ways of the Sephardim, still the predominate tradition in Skopje today.

At the end of the seventeenth century the Jewish community, under Ottoman rule, had grown to some 3,000 members with two synagogues, Beit Aron and Beit Yaacov. Generally, the Jews were left alone, were able to conduct their own internal matters and lived a relatively peaceful existence as miners, spinners, traders of cotton and wheat, small store owners and street peddlers. They were, however, subjected to an inordinate number of special taxes that only they had to pay, such as a tax on the clothes they wore in the army and one for kosher meat. The Skopje community was always poor. Commercial enterprise was quite nominal in this rural area and largely dominated by the peasants that were either Turkish, Armenian, Serbian, Macedonian, Gypsy, Bulgarian or Wallachian. The economic status of the community did not change a great deal when Yugoslavia became a country after World War I. The Jewish community reached its largest size at 4,000 in 1940.

War came to Skopje in April, 1941, when the Germans occupied the city. Soon afterwards, the Bulgarian fascists were given control of all of Macedonia. Immediately, Jewish life began to deteriorate, with Jewish shops and homes being plundered, Jews being publicly humiliated in the streets and individuals randomly killed. The noose around the Jewish ghetto became tighter and tighter. Finally, SS Attaché Dannecker and the Bulgarian government agreed: the Jews would be rounded up and deported to Poland. On March 10th and 11th, 1943, orders were given to bring all of the Jews from throughout Macedonia to Skopje. In Skopje, they were taken as prisoners to Monopol and kept there until the Germans decided when and where they would be sent.

Before the war, twenty-five percent of Yugoslavia's cigarettes were made at this factory— Monopol. All of the local tobacco factories came under one management system and, thus, created a monopoly in Skopje; hence, the name Monopol from the word monopoly would soon have only one meaning for the Jews of Macedonia. Altogether, 7,215 Jews were kept in the tobacco drying rooms. All the windows were sealed and covered with dark cloth so no outside light could enter. Prisoners were forced to sleep crowded together on the wooden slats with only fifty centimeters for each person, without blankets in the cold damp rooms. There were no toilet facilities for the prisoners and very little food. In the small antechamber next to the large drying room, the women were taken by the Bulgarian officers to be raped and humiliated. This torture ended when the transports to Treblinka began on March 22, 1943. None of those deported survived. The only Jews from Skopje to survive the Holocaust were those few who were taken as P.O.W.s from the Yugoslavian army or those who made it to the mountains and joined the partisans.

After the war, Jewish life was slowly reconstructed. Jews from throughout the country came to live in Skopje, certain to get jobs. In 1963, the city once again was devastated, this time from a tremendous earthquake that killed thousands, including several Jews, and destroyed the community's only synagogue, which was never rebuilt. The few religious articles that were saved are kept in a glass case in the Jewish community center's office.

Today, there are only eighty two Jews in all of Macedonia. Only one lives in Štip and one in Gevgelija. Of the eighty Jews in Skopje, only seven to ten are originally from there. Though the community is small and isolated, there seems to be an incredible will to survive among the Jews I met there. Below are excerpts from two of those people I met: Žaklina and her wonderful, warm grandfather, Benjamin Samokovlija, the former president of the community.

Mr. Samokovlija: "I was born and raised in Sarajevo. In our home Spanish (Judeo-Spanish) was our first language. When walking in the streets of the old market place, you could hear the language everywhere, even from many of the gentile shopkeepers. Sarajevo was a vibrant Jewish community. I tried to take full advantage of everything there was. I was in the Lyra Choir, where I learned many beautiful Spanish songs. I also played football (soccer) on the Maccabi team and was an active member of Hashomer-Ha-Tzair (Hebrew: Young Guardians, Socialist-Zionist movement). When the Germans came in 1941, I immediately joined the partisans. In 1943, I was captured and taken prisoner. The Germans first sent me to a camp in Bosnia, then to a labor camp called Pavle Melas, which was near Saloniki. At this camp my friend and I were the only Jews, but they did not know we were Jewish. We worked repairing the electrical systems on the trains. One day I was shocked to hear some Spanish being spoken; it was coming from a train that had arrived the night before. The train was filled with Greek Jews from the south and the islands. Of course I understood everything that

was being said, but I did not dare take a chance to speak with them. They were moaning and crying for water and some food. Later that afternoon, I was able to bring them a little of what I had; it was not much. That evening the train continued on to Treblinka with its human cargo. The next day some Austrian SS Gestapo were inspecting the camp. One of the chief commandants came over to me while I was working. He slapped my shoulder and said, 'Du bist a Jude.' (You are a Jew.) I ignored him, pretending I did not understand German. Again, he slapped me and said the same thing. Finally, I turned around and saw this sneering, clean-shaven, well-dressed officer glaring at me. I said to him in broken German, 'Anshuldig mein Herr ich bin a Serb fun Bosnia.' (Excuse me, sir. I am a Serb, from Bosnia.) He insisted I was a Jew, spat on the ground and resolutely walked away. That afternoon, a kapo came up to me and told me I had to report to the commandant's office first thing tomorrow morning. It was their way of saying I was being transferred to the north—to the death camps. With the help of Macedonian partisans, I escaped that very evening and stayed with them, fighting in Greece to the end of the war. My friend had been taken to another barrack and I wasn't able to get to him. He was shot while being transferred to the north. The commandant who slapped my shoulder and gave the order for me to be sent to my death—Kurt Waldheim."

Žaklina: "When I went to school I was alone, the only Jew in the entire school. So, going to the Jewish camp in Pirovac has been very important for me over the years. I have been going since I was ten years old and now have friends from all over the country. Pirovac is extremely important because it is a place where we can meet and do things in a Jewish milieu with kids our own age. Here in Skopje we are few, but I am an optimist. If we want to accomplish something, all we need are the people to come to the Jewish club. There are eight young people between the ages of 16–24 years that come regularly, every Friday evening. On the Jewish festivals we have about thirty Jews and some non-Jews at the club. The non-Jews come because they are interested in this culture they know little about. The parents prepare special foods and we provide different cultural programs. Last year I formed a drama group called Magen David. It is a member of the League for Amateur Troupes here in Skopje. We are seventeen in the troupe, some of whom are not Jewish, like our music director—who is a Gypsy. We do everything ourselves—like my mother, who makes the costumes. Last year we wrote a play called Purim and performed it to great success in all the Jewish clubs in the country. We hope to be able to go to Israel someday with the troupe. Our drama group, club activities, Jewish seminars—which are held in a different city every year—and the Maccabi sport festival on the seaside are all activities in which we from Skopje participate. We are a few here, but we are committed to our Jewish heritage."

Skopje: Žaklina Risteska and her mother, Laura Dukič-Samokovlija, who regularly visited the camp in Pirovac and was known as Tetka (Aunt) Laura.

Sarajevo: The Gaon brothers, Jakub and Jeroham.

Sarajevo: The office of the Jewish community.

Split: The office of the Jewish community.

Skopje: Benjamin Samokovlija, the former president of the Jewish community.

Skopje: Žaklina Risteska (l) and her friend, Šaska Mladenovska, represent the few Jewish youth still living in Skopje.

Sarajevo: The Ashkenazic synagogue is today the focal point of the Jewish community. Built in 1902, the Moorish-style structure being renovated by the state.

Split: The interior of the
Ashkenazic synagogue, built
in the mid-18th century.

Sarajevo: Interior
f the Ashkenazic
synagogue.

Sarajevo: The Sephardic synagogue, built in 1581, today houses the Jewish Museum.

Split: Eduard Tauber, the president of the Jewish community.

Sarajevo: A plaque in Serbo-Croatian reads:
*This memorial tablet will be an eternal reminder of the existence of the burial society and Chief Rabbi Samuel Weszel. Our thoughts will be with him forever. We beg that our souls will be forgiven.*
Tishri, 5691–September, 1931.

Sarajevo: The vandalized, unused khadar-tahora, located in the cemetery. The Hebrew inscription on the front facade says: *Bless the court of truth.*

Sarajevo: Peasants are permitted to harvest the wild grass and wheat for their own use in exchange for maintaining the grounds of the Mt. Trebevic Jewish cemetery, founded in 1630.

Sarajevo: An evening picnic in the Jewish cemetery.

Sarajevo: A broken
window of the khadar-
tahora revealing a view
of the city below.

Sarajevo: The interior of the khadar-tahora (Heb. purification room). The Hebrew inscription on the wall says:
*God gives and God takes, may his name the Lord be blessed.*

Split: The synagogue's memorial plaque reads: *In remembrance of the young Jews of Split who gave their lives in the war as partisans under Tito. The first to be sacrificed by the Fascists was Viktor Torfono.*

Sarajevo: Standing on the location where their first synagogue was built, this monument commemorates the 400th anniversary of the first Jewish community in Bosnia-Hercegovina.

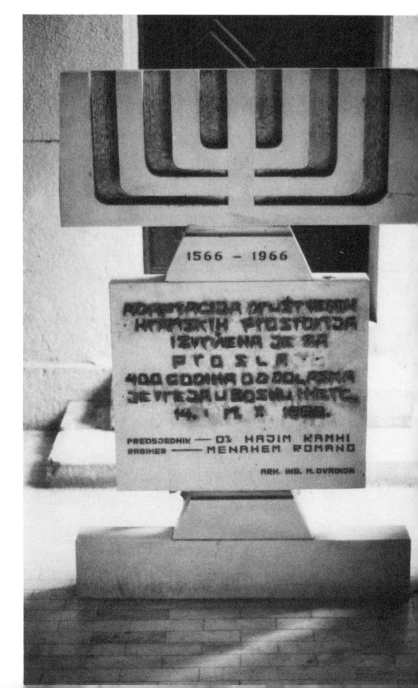

Split: The Jewish cemetery, founded in 1573, is located on Mt. Marjan, which overlooks the city and the Adriatic Sea.

Skopje: A memorial, placed in the Jewish cemetery for those who were shot in Skopje or murdered in the concentration camps.

Skopje: The drying rooms for the tobacco leaves, in which Jews were held prisoner.

Skopje: Near the former Monopol Prison,
train tracks lead to Treblinka.

Pirovac: A lecture on Jewish customs given by the assistant camp director.

Pirovac: Fun and games in the dormitory.

Pirovac: Celebrating Shabbat at camp.

Pirovac: Cooling off in the river.

Split: Children stand in the former
Jewish Quarter. Note the empty slot
where the mezuzzah was once inserted
into the stone doorpost.

# *Bulgaria*

Archeological records indicate the presence of Jews in Bulgaria as early as the second century. Ruins of a synagogue near Nikopol and letters sent by Emperor Theodosius I to the governors of Thrace and Illyria in the fourth century mention the persecution of the Jews and the destruction of their synagogues.

After the barbarian invasion of Bulgaria in the fifth and sixth centuries, there are no records of Jews being in the country until the eighth century, when Jewish refugees from Byzantium and Thessaloniki fled to Bulgaria. During the reign of Bulgarian Czar Boris I (852–89), there was much religious unrest and the Jews tried to take advantage of the situation and began proselytizing among the adulterous Bulgarians. Though the Christian missionaries were more successful, the Bulgarians accepted a combination of pagan, Christian and Jewish rituals and beliefs. Many Bulgarian princes had Jewish names, such as Aaron, Moses, David, Samuel and Joseph.

During the Crusades, many Jews fleeing Central Europe found refuge in Bulgaria. After it became independent of Byzantium rule, Jews were invited to help establish commercial and financial centers in the country. Soon afterwards, Czar Ivan Alexander (1331–71) married a Jewish woman named Sarah. Upon her baptism (1345), she took the name of Theodora. The Czarina used her position to considerably influence the government's positive treatment on behalf of the Jews. But, again, the Christian clergy grew angry at the favorable treatment and growing influence of the Jews and had restrictions imposed on the Jewish populace.

Until the fifteenth century, the largest segment of Bulgaria's Jews belonged to the Romaniot Jewish rite, with their own synagogues and many of their own customs, including bigamy. The Romaniot Jews rarely spoke Bulgarian, choosing instead to speak Greek.

When Bulgaria became part of the Ottoman Empire in 1396, Jews were living throughout the country. At this time, there were three distinct Jewish communities: the Romaniot, the Ashkenazim who had primarily come from Bavaria (1470) and Hungary (1376), and the Sephardim (1391). The Ashkenazim had their own synagogues and spoke Yiddish among themselves. By the end of the fifteenth century, thousands of Sephardim escaping the Inquisitions in the Iberian peninsula found refuge in Bulgaria. After 1640, the three separate Jewish communities merged, adopting for the most part the customs and language of the Sephardim. The Romaniot distinction disappeared, but the Ashkenazim still maintained their own rituals and prayers in the synagogues. The Jewish community grew and was relatively prosperous for the next 482 years of Ottoman rule.

When the Bulgarians began agitating for independence, the Jews joined their fellow countrymen and fought alongside the Bulgarians against the Turkish. Finally, in 1878, Bulgaria gained its independence. With the signing of the Berlin Treaty of 1878, Jews and other minorities in the Balkans were granted full emancipation and ensured equal rights. However, as in other countries in the region, many peasants remained anti-Semitic and made it difficult for the Jews to obtain land. Despite problems in the rural countryside and the anti-Semitism pervasive in the political parties in the urban centers, Jews were able to maintain a thriving and cohesive community. They organized various social, cultural, religious and political groups. The Zionist groups were founded in the early 1880s and became the most influential in Bulgaria in the mid-1930s on matters of daily Jewish life. Jewish culture reached its zenith in Bulgaria in the mid-1930s, when there were nearly 50,000 Jews, most of them living in Sofia.

The relatively tranquil times for the Jews came to an abrupt end in February 1940, with the appointment of Bogdan Filov as Premier. A noted Germanophile, he directed, with the consent of King Boris III, the passage of *The Law for the Protection of the Nation* through the parliament in January of 1941. The drafting of the law was based upon Germany's Nuremberg Laws and severely restricted the Jews' legal rights and social relations with their fellow Bulgarians. Some Bulgarians saw this as an opportunity to take advantage of the Jews' economic deprivations, but the majority of the people were decisively against the law. The anti-Jewish laws included a special tax on Jewish-owned property, a curfew, the confiscation of personal and business telephones and radios and the mandatory wearing of the yellow Star of David on the outside of a Jew's clothing.

At this time the monarchy was quite weak, trying to stave off both its extremely poor public opinion in the cities and the Bulgarian communist insurgents in the countryside. On March 1, 1941, the Bulgarian government officially joined the Axis powers and pinned their hopes for survival on the success of the Third Reich.

In 1942, the issue of rounding up and deporting the Jews came to the forefront when SS Attaché Theodor Dannecker, a confidant of Adolf Eichmann, arrived in Sofia to meet the King. Under pressure from certain cabinet members—and realizing the resistance the people would mete out against the government—the King agreed to deport only 20,000 Jews from newly occupied Thrace and Macedonia. The majority of these Jews—Yugoslavian and Greek—died in Treblinka. Soon afterwards, the Germans pressured the King to send 8,000 Jews to the interior of the country, where their deportation to Poland would not be so noticeable. The public quickly found out and, along with the church, organized huge public protests against the movement. With continued pressure, including the deputy vice president of the parliament and the archbishop, no additional Jews were deported. Ironically, at the same time the Germans were pressuring for the deportation of Bulgaria's Jews, the government agreed to allow four thousand children and four hundred elderly Jews to leave for Palestine. The request came from the British government, with mediation from the Swiss government.

After a meeting with Hitler in Berlin in March of 1943, King Boris III agreed to set up country-side labor camps which were to pave the way for future deportations. All Jewish men up to the age of fifty were taken to labor camps, one of which was near the town of Trăn, near the Yugoslavian border. But again, with the support of the majority of the Bulgarian people, none were ever deported outside of the country. Bulgarian Jews were the only Jews in occupied Europe to be spared the horror of the concentration camps.

Tragically, however, the government allowed the Nazis to transport thousands of Greek Jews through western Bulgaria on their way to the crematoriums in Poland.

After the war, emigration to Israel became the prime objective of the Jewish community. Between 1948 and 1951, 44,267 Jews immigrated to Israel. Beginning in the late 40s, and continuing through the 50s, it became quite difficult for those Jews who remained in Bulgaria to keep a strong Jewish identity. Jewish schools and hospitals were closed due to their small numbers and pressure from the communist government. For the next thirty years, Jewish life consisted mainly of a few elderly Jews going to the synagogues and Jewish clubs that were allowed to remain open. It was not until recent changes in the government — due to perestroika — that the Jewish youth have begun to take an active role in the community.

Today, the Jewish community is largely Sephardic, with nearly eighty percent of the country's 4,000 Jews living in Sofia. Jewish life has dramatically grown, with much of the current activity centering around the celebration of the 500th anniversary of the expulsion of the Jews from Spain.

Ironically, in spite of their new freedoms, many of the young Jews are opting to emigrate to Israel instead of facing a ten to fifteen year struggle for a stable and viable economy in Bulgaria. This new wave of emigration is severely diminishing the Jewish community of its future leaders, raising strong doubts as to its survival into the 21st century.

# SOFIA

When the Roman empire split in 293 C.E. the territories of the east Mediterranean became known as the Byzantine Empire, and the Jews of Sofia belonged to the sect called the Romaniot. The Romaniot were joined by the Ashkenazim, who fled Central Europe in the fifteenth century, and then, finally, by the Sephardim a few years later.

Due to the close proximity and trade contacts with the nearby Sephardic communities, the Sephardim of Sofia quickly became the major and most influential of the three separate Jewish communities.

Up to the mid-nineteenth century the Jews worked as artisans and businessmen. They enjoyed the economic power that came from being the transit center for commerce from Thessaloniki to Belgrade and Istanbul to Bucharest. In 1850 the community numbered 3,000.

When Bulgaria defeated Turkey in 1878, the Jewish community was praised highly by the new government for their defense of the city, particularly for the way they guarded the city against fire.

The Jewish community continued to grow with an influx of Russian Jews escaping the rabid anti-Semitism in the early years of the twentieth century. In the 1920s through mid-30s, thousands of Jews from the former territories of the Ottoman Empire in Asia Minor settled in Sofia.

By 1940, the community had grown to 29,000. Life for these Jews during the next four-and-a-half years came to mean fear and caution, as the Bulgarian government joined the Axis powers. Despite the pro-German position of the government, the anti-Jewish laws, and the dispersal of Jews, earmarked for deportation, to the countryside, the general public did not allow their fellow countrymen to be exterminated by the Germans or fascist Bulgarian army.

Between 1948 and 1951, 24,000 Jews emigrated to Israel. For those who remained, there was an active secular life in Sofia throughout the forties to mid-fifties. There was a Jewish restaurant, drama group, choir, dance troupe called "Sadikov," two Jewish schools and a Jewish hospital. This Jewish activity came to an abrupt end in 1956, when the Bulgarian government turned conspicuously pro-Arab after the defeat of Egypt by Israel during the Sinai War. Soon afterwards, a government-authorized Jewish organization was established called The Socialist Cultural and Educational Association of Jews in the People's Republic of Bulgaria. The hand-picked staff became servants of the government, closing down all the Jewish cultural, religious and philanthropic organizations and turning over to the government all the community's buildings, including the schools and hospital. In 1961, only the Jewish Cultural House and the synagogue were retained by the community.

Jewish religious life never regained the strength and influence in Sofia it had before the war. Most of the Jews who remained in Bulgaria were communists with little interest in organized religion. The last rabbi in Bulgaria, Chief Rabbi Asher Hananel, tried to keep the synagogue open, but was repeatedly harassed by government authorities. In 1956, he was arrested and put into prison, accused of black marketing. Finally, in 1961, he was rearrested for refusing to close the synagogue. He died in prison in 1962.

On January 26, 1990, Jewish life, virtually dormant for thirty years, blossomed once again in Sofia. On that day, the Jewish club "Shalom" officially began. Before the recent political changes many of the same people who are now involved in "Shalom" met clandestinely on a regular basis at various homes to celebrate Jewish holidays and talk about Jewish problems. The members of "Shalom" meet every Friday night in the Jewish Cultural House to socialize, organize lectures and concerts, and celebrate Jewish festivals. Currently, they are busy preparing for various events and exhibitions that will take place in Sofia during 1992, when the 500th anniversary of the Sephardic presence in the country is observed.

A group of high school and university students insisted on forming their own organization because they did not trust some of the older members in "Shalom" who were open proponents of the previous communist regime. Their organization is called "Irgun." It has specifically been involved in organizing the Ulpanim (Hebrew language courses) where there are now one hundred and fifty students and teachers from Bulgaria and Israel. "Irgun" is also active in programing cultural events geared for the youth and organizing trips to Israel.

Many of the young Jews I met who were in "Irgun" are moving—or planning to move—to Israel. Some are leaving for Zionist reasons, others for economic ones. If, for whatever reason, any Jew returns to Bulgaria after having immigrated to Israel, they are allowed to return. Before the recent political changes Jews were allowed to leave for Israel, but their choice was a permanent one. This, of course, put strain on people who wanted to immigrate to Israel but had older parents who did not want to leave Bulgaria. Ironically, this new freedom has created a swell in the numbers of young Jews leaving for Israel and the current Jewish leadership is worried. With the attrition rate so high, they feel that in ten to twenty years the most active Jewish organization will be the one providing assistance for the elderly Jews.

The enthusiasm, energy and ideas are at a high level, but financial resources are limited. The Jewish community is currently trying to reclaim some thirty properties that were originally theirs, but were confiscated. These properties would provide, through rents, some much needed income.

One Friday evening, as I was visiting the "Shalom" club, a forty-two year old man left me with this poignant statement:

"Four centuries ago Bulgarian Jews and non-Jews helped the wandering Sephardim to find a new home and relieved them of their pain. Now, this rich legacy of our past to the present and for the future is a thin unraveling thread. Maybe the Jews of the world will have compassion and help us in this time of need."

# PLOVDIV

A few years ago in Plovdiv (ancient Philippopolis), archaeologists unearthed parts of a mosaic floor and panels depicting a menorah. They were parts of a synagogue that had stood in 290 C.E., built by Jewish tradesman and craftsmen who had come from Palestine and Syria searching for trade routes along the Maritsa River that passed through Thrace on its way into the Aegean Sea.

Plovdiv suffered many sacks during the Middle Ages and Jews, who were blamed for the city's woes, often suffered harassment. When the Ottoman Empire took control in 1364, however, the Jewish community enjoyed many years of relative peace. As an agricultural region, the city prospered on the Belgrade-Sofia-Istanbul trade route and the Jews prospered as well.

In 1786, Rabbi Abraham ibn Aroiio (1750–1819) led the building of the first synagogue since that small, ancient one and named it Beit Yeshurun.

After the Russo-Turkish War of 1877–1878, Plovdiv became the capital of the Turkish vassal state of Eastern Rumelia. Jews were a major part of the vassal assembly, voting predominantly for the Bulgarian Party, which led to the annexation of Eastern Rumelia by Bulgaria in 1885.

With the coming of the twentieth century, the Jewish community became consumed with Zionism. In 1924 the national Zionist headquarters was placed in Plovdiv. They proceeded to print *Hashofar,* the largest Zionist newspaper in the country until the war began.

With the dawn of 1941 came anti-Jewish laws, including the mandatory wearing of the yellow Star of David badge. SS Attaché Theodor Dannecker soon gave the deportation orders. All the Jewish unemployed, sick and elderly were sent to buildings in Sofia designed by the huge Star of David banners hung on the outside walls. Prior to World War II, Plovdiv had the second largest Jewish community in Bulgaria, numbering 6,500. Again, the determination and will of the Bulgarian people to thwart any attempt to deport the Jews of Plovdiv from Bulgaria saved the entire community.

After the war, Plovdiv still had an active Jewish community containing five synagogues, a school (which existed until 1949), a Maccabi sports club, a cultural center known as Sholom Aleichem and an extremely active Zionist organization "Hashomer Hatzair." In 1950 the community's numbers had been halved by immigration to Israel. In 1967 there were only 1,000 Jews left. Today, the community numbers about four hundred.

Today, a Beit Midrash (Hebrew: small house of study) and the lone city synagogue Beit Knesset Zion stand in the former Jewish quarters. Inside the courtyard stands a large, six-story apartment complex built on the site of the former synagogue Beit Yeshurun, which the government razed in 1965. The Jewish community could no longer afford the upkeep of the synagogue and, with a diminishing population, could not justify keeping the doors of three houses of worship open when they could barely get a minyan at one on Shabbat. In return for the land, the government built the apartments and gave the Jewish community first choice in obtaining apartments. Today, about sixty percent of the community live in these apartments.

Until recently, there was a young khazan (cantor) in the community, but, like many other Jews before him, he immigrated to Israel. Even without a rabbi or khazan, there are still prayer services every erev Shabbat and on the holidays. The new democratic changes in the government and the reestablishment of diplomatic ties between Bulgaria and Israel have infused the small Jewish community with new energy. Fifty young people meet on a regular basis at the Sholom Aleichem club and participate in Hebrew classes and other activities.

However, with every passing year, the Jewish community becomes a little smaller, with aliya and assimilation being the major culprits.

Josef and Kristina Djaldety are representative of a typical Jewish family living in Plovdiv today. Josef was born in Dolna Banya, a village in the middle of the Borovec mountains west of Plovdiv. When he was a young boy in the 1930s, he and his family moved to Plovdiv, where he grew up in a traditional Jewish home. Both his parents spoke Judeo-Spanish as their first language. Josef's father was a waiter at a cafe frequented by the town's artists, while his mother worked as a seamstress. They were poor, but they would have been poorer if they had stayed in Dolna Banya where the main source of income was farming. Josef's father was not a farmer. When World War II began, Josef, along with the other young Jewish males of Plovdiv, was arrested and scheduled for deportation to a forced labor camp near the Yugoslavian border. The police let it be known that the men could be released if a ransom was paid, but most of the Jews were poor after having much of their property and savings already confiscated. Finally, they pooled their resources together and paid the ransom.

Soon after the men were released in the spring of 1944 the fascist organization Bran-Nitzi formed a ghetto for the Jews of Plovdiv and the surrounding outlying areas. One day Josef was caught walking in the ghetto without his yellow Star of David badge. The police immediately stopped him and began to beat him severely. A friend quickly ran over and paid the police to stop. Though he had been warned, Josef often continued to openly defy the fascist authorities. Luckily, six months later, on September 8, 1944, the war ended for him when the Russians moved into Bulgaria.

After the war, Josef married Kristina, a gentile, and began to train to be an opera singer. Once accepted to the Plovdiv Opera, he traveled the world, while Kristina raised their two sons in a Jewish home. Today, Josef is retired and lives with his wife in a small, neat home next to the synagogue courtyard—where the community's shokhet (Hebrew: ritual slaughterer) once lived and koshered poultry. Josef's two sons married non-Jews and live in Plovdiv.

While walking to catch the train which I would take back to Sofia, Josef left me with this stirring reminder about these shrinking remnant Sephardic communities:

"My daughter-in-laws keep the Jewish traditions better than my sons—just as my wife did. I hope they go to Israel because this country can't give them what they should have in their lifetime. I'll miss them. Soon there will be no one to bury us, say kaddish or put flowers on our graves."

Plovdiv: Prayers are held every Friday evening at the Beit Midrash (Heb. small house of study), as well as on Jewish holidays.

Plovdiv: Abraham Saul Bechar, president of the Jewish community, leaving the synagogue.

David Kahan, shamash, opening the doors of the
abandoned Beit Zion synagogue.

Sofia: The Selictar family (left to right): Liko, Viza, Vitali and Tania, standing outside the Jewish Cultural House.

Sofia: The shamash (sexton) waits for Friday evening services to begin.

Plovdiv: The front doors leading to the courtyard of the former Karlovo synagogue, named for the Jews originating from a small town at the foot of the Rhodope mountains.

Plovdiv: A war memorial plaque in the closed Beit Zion synagogue reads: *These are the names of our heroic brothers who spilled their blood to protect our country Bulgaria and honored our people in the Balkan and World War, 1912–1918.*

Plovdiv: Many partisan memorial plaques, such as this one to a young Jew, Marko Joshua Dekala, nicknamed Krasni (Red), have been placed in front of partisans' former homes throughout the city.

Sofia: A state-run hospital, this former Jewish hospital was seized by the government in 1950. Ownership of many Jewish properties seized between 1947 and 1952 are presently in dispute.

Plovdiv: The Maccabi sports club before the Holocaust. Today, it is used for the local sports club.

Sofia: The interior of the synagogue, which has been closed to the public for ten years because of renovations. The Hebrew inscription above the Ark reads: *Know who you stand before.*

Plovdiv: The interior of the unused Beit Zion synagogue.

Sofia: A young girl lighting a candle in memory of loved ones and asking God to ward off impending danger. The bowl, known as the second Ner Tamid, is a Sephardic tradition only in the Balkans.

Sofia: Beit Knesset Sofia, built in 1909 and seating 2,000, is today the largest Sephardic synagogue in the world.

Sofia: Maxim Kohen, the assistant cantor, leading Friday evening services.

Sofia: Cantor Khaim Meshulam leading the "sheloshim" (Heb. thirty) services for the Yulzari family one month after the death of the mother.

Sofia: The grave of Heski Levi, a classical violinist. Note the shifting and sinking graves.

Sofia: The grave of Jewish communist Aron Mois Koen
*He gave his life for the struggle against fascism.*

Sofia: Bulgarian Rom (Gypsies)
remodeling the khadar-tahorah
located in the Jewish cemetery.

Sofia: Clara Armandova, a well-known Bulgarian singer and actress, gives Judeo-Spanish folk song concerts throughout Europe.

Sofia: An afternoon of backgammon at the Jewish Club.

Plovdiv: Josef and Kristina Djaldety standing in front of their home in the synagogue courtyard.

Sofia: Enjoying the kiddush (Heb. a small meal served after prayers) in the synagogue.

Sofia: The lady shamash (female sexton) helps at various jobs in the synagogue. Her main duty is lighting the Shabbat candles every Friday at sundown.

Sofia: The cantor kisses the mezuzzah as he leaves the synagogue.

# *Turkey*

When we speak about Turkey today, we are speaking about a relatively young republic, founded after the Balkan and first World War in 1924. A unique country, Turkey is the strategic bridge between Europe and Asia. For centuries the country has stood at the crossroads of Western and Eastern cultural influences.

The history of the Jews in Turkey goes back much further than 1924, beginning at the time of the Second Temple, when the region was ruled by the Greeks and Romans. In the seventh century the eastern sector of the Roman Empire broke away, converted to Christianity and became known as Byzantium. Under their Byzantium rulers, the Jews had a precarious existence, repeatedly forced to become baptized, forbidden to practice Judaism, unable to build new synagogues and often restricted in their travel. Consequently, many Jews sought refuge in North Africa, Palestine and in the Crimea area.

In 1326 Sultan Urhan captured Bursa and made it the capital of the emerging Ottoman Empire. He encouraged the Jews to settle in the sultanate and own land and houses. Gradually, the Ottoman Empire captured more territory and, by 1500, the empire's borders were as far west as Algeria, as far south as Yemen, as far north as southern Ukraine and as far east as the Persian Gulf. When the Jews were expelled from the Iberian peninsula, the Sultan of Turkey, Bayezid II (1481–1512), openly invited the Sephardic Jews to settle in the Ottoman empire. He felt they would enrich the arts and sciences, trade and industry, diplomacy and administration. The new immigrants brought, among other things, the use of gunpowder and the manufacture of the cannon.

"I am amazed with those who say Ferdinand of Spain is clever, since he is impoverishing his country and enriching my lands," he exclaimed.

The sultan had another reason for openly accepting the Jews. He wanted them to act as a check and balance vis-a-vis the Christians in the empire he did not trust.

In the late seventeenth century, thousands of

Ashkenazim fleeing Bogdan Chmielnicki and his marauding cossack hordes from Poland and the Ukraine came to the Ottoman lands. In 1660, the Jewish population in the Ottoman Empire swelled to over one million.

So determined were the Sephardic émigrés in maintaining their Spanish-Jewish heritage in the Ottoman lands that those Jewish communities that existed before they arrived—Romaniot, Ashkenazim and Italian—were quickly absorbed into Sephardic culture. Consequently, Judeo-Spanish became the mother tongue of Jews living in the lands bordering the Mediterranean and Aegean Seas.

The high status of Turkish Jewry was reflected in the appointment and influence of the imperial chief rabbi, known as the Hakham Bashi. The Hakham Bashi had the same authority and public stature as the Moslem kadi (judge) and was higher than the Greek Patriarch. The Hakham Bashi was—and still is—chosen by the Jewish community.

Despite the relative calm the Jews enjoyed, they were often reminded that they were still subject to the whims of the ruling families in Constantinople. Poverty and religious intolerance wrecked havoc upon the Jews even in the Ottoman lands. But, during the Ottoman Empire's reign, no country in Europe allowed the Jewish mind and spirit such freedom. At the beginning of the nineteenth century, some of the most prominent centers of Jewish life and scholarship were in the Ottoman empire: in Izmir (Smyrna), Istanbul, Thessaloniki, Sarajevo, Rhodes and Edirne (Adrianople).

The disintegration (Balkanization) of the Ottoman empire beginning in the mid-nineteenth century through the end of World War II found many Sephardim living in new independent countries: Bulgaria, Albania, Rumania, Yugoslavia, Greece and Turkey. Each country had its own treatment regarding its Jewish minority.

During the inter-war years, the spirit of a new Turkish nationalism, known as the Young Turk Movement, was on the rise. This movement spurred new secular reforms introduced by the first president of the new Turkish republic, Kemal Atatürk, whereby all minorities were to be treated equally. Certain privileges the Jews had under the Sultan—such as separate Hebrew schools—were now abolished. Gradually, the Jewish community looked less to the government for assistance and began to become self-sufficient and rather insular—a characteristic still felt in the Istanbul Jewish community.

As anti-Semitic sentiment swept Europe in the late 1930s, life became increasingly more difficult for the neutral Turkish Jews. Policy dealing with the Jews varied depending on government expediency. Before and during World War II, Turkey solicited and welcomed leading Jewish scientists, scholars and artists fleeing Nazi-occupied countries. Many became professors in the universities, while others were allowed transit en route to Palestine. In 1941, the Turkish consulate went to Paris to ensure that all Jews holding Turkish passports would be allowed to transit safely through Europe back to Turkey. The Turkish government also saved all Jews holding Turkish passports who were on the island of Rhodes, but callously allowed the Germans to deport the Greek Jews to concentration camps in Poland.

On the other hand, when, in the beginning of the war, it seemed that the Axis powers were edging close to victory, the majority of the native Turkish Jews were treated harshly. Taxes that were justified as wartime needs fell especially hard on Jews, becoming so inordinately high that many were bankrupt. A pro-Axis press eagerly created a hysteria denouncing the Jews as disloyal, "a people with alien blood." Many were arrested and their property seized. Many were added to other minorities temporarily deported to Thrace and the Dardanelles area. In 1944, when the tide of the war turned drastically against Germany and defeat loomed near, the Turkish government passed a law, releasing all debtors from prison and canceling all unpaid taxes.

After the war, Jewish life improved. With the establishment of the State of Israel, the Turkish government allowed the emigration of its Jews to Israel. Nearly fifty percent of the 76,965 Jews living in Turkey after the war emigrated to Israel between 1948 and 1950. In the ensuing years, Turkish officials made it difficult for the Jews to emigrate to Israel, openly arguing that the exodus undermined the economy. Quietly, they wished to appease neighboring Arab countries, as well as their own Moslem citizens.

The rise of militant Islam and the frightening terrorist attack on the Neve Shalom synagogue in Istanbul in September of 1986, which resulted in twenty one worshippers killed and dozens of others wounded, made the Jewish community tense and introverted. Even so, the community's deep pride in its Jewish heritage has made it the strongest culturally and religiously in the Balkans today. In fact, during recent years, while Israel has been plagued with intense political and economic problems, many Turkish Jews have left Israel and returned to Turkey, where daily life is much easier for them.

At the present time, there are some 22,000 Jews living in Turkey, primarily in Istanbul, with fewer in Izmir and ever fewer in Ankara, Adana and Edirne. Old age, a low birth rate and immigration to the United States have caused a gradual erosion of the Jewish populace. But, except for Spain's, Turkey retains the most stable Sephardic community I visited.

Unlike the Sephardim in Spain and Portugal, the Turkish Jews will not commemorate, but celebrate their fortunate and illustrious history achieved five hundred years after they were expelled from the Iberian peninsula.

Istanbul: The former Jewish school in the Kuzguncuk district, founded in 1923.

# ISTANBUL

Jews have lived in and around Istanbul, formerly known as Constantinople, for over one thousand years. But the city did not become a magnet for Jews until Mohammad II, the Conqueror (1451–81), captured Istanbul (the name the Ottomans gave to the city) from the Byzantine Empire and made it the capital. In order to renovate the conquered city, Muslims, Christians and Jews from throughout the empire were encouraged to settle. Jews responded—coming primarily from Thessaloniki, Bulgaria, Macedonia and Albania—settling along both sides of the Golden Horn strait. They settled in the districts of Balat, Galata, Hasköy, Ortaköy, and across the Bosporus in Üsküdar in the Kuzguncuk district.

The Jews of Istanbul were divided among the Romaniots, the former inhabitants of Greece and Byzantium; the Ashkenazim; Italians and Sephardim. The Ashkenazim came in two major waves. The first wave, in the fifteenth century, were Jews from the Hungarian lands conquered by sultan Suleiman the Magnificent. The second group, in the sixteenth century, were from Bavaria, expelled by King Ludwig IX. The largest of these refugee groups were the Sephardim who had been expelled from the Iberian peninsula at the end of the fifteenth century.

Each sect vigorously maintained their own separate community, including its own synagogue, rabbi, melamed (Hebrew teacher), Talmud Torah, Khevra Kaddishe (burial society), welfare societies and shokhet (ritual slaughterer). By the middle of the sixteenth century, the Sephardim, due to their prolific numbers, strong economic status and cultural fortitude were the most influential sect among the 50,000 Jews of Istanbul.

The economic, social, cultural and religious life for the Jews reached such a high level during the sixteenth century that Istanbul became one of the most important Jewish cities in the world. Some of the people who helped to create this thriving and enlightened community were physicians from the Hamon family who served Bayezid II, Selim I and Suleim II. The Mendes family, originally Conversos, were financiers from Portugal. João Micas, who officially converted to Judaism, changed his name to Joseph Nasi, became close friends with Selim II and wielded great influence, especially on Jewish policies. The Jewish community also took great pride in their Hebrew printing establishments. Between the sixteenth and eighteenth centuries, Istanbul was the center of Hebrew printing in the Ottoman empire. Some of the better known printers were David and Samuel ibn Nehemias, exiles from Spain, and the Soncino family, originally from Italy.

The seventeenth and eighteenth centuries brought a gradual decline in the economic and cultural status of the Jewish community. The Ottoman empire had its hands full staving off the many internal uprisings in its vast territories. Many huge fires in these years had destroyed many of the Jewish quarters; and the arrest and subsequent downfall of the false messiah Shabbatai Tzvi caused embarrassment and persecution for his Jewish adherents.

In the nineteenth century, the Jewish community was reorganized under the leadership of the hakham bashi (chief rabbi). This office was instituted in 1836 and still continues today. Under the hakham bashi a religious council and a secular council existed. The religious council consisted of twelve rabbis, four of which were appointed Chief Rabbi of a specific district. Under each of these four rabbis were local rabbis who headed their synagogue administration and religious duties.

The secular council usually consisted of Jewish officials of the government who came from prominent wealthy families. All religious matters were taken to the Chief Rabbis, who headed up the Beit Dinim (House of Laws), while all other matters Jewish and non-Jewish were brought first to the secular council. If they could not solve the matter, then the plaintiffs were brought before the courts of the state. These regulations were kept in place until the formation of the Republic of Turkey in 1923. At the community's apex, these councils served nearly 100,000 Jews prior to World War I.

During the 1920s and 30s, the Jewish community in Istanbul came under pressure to abandon its religious autonomy. Jewish schools had to teach in Turkish, not in French or in Hebrew, and religious instruction was forbidden. French had been the primary language of the upper class Jews and in all the Alliance Israélite Universelle Schools throughout the Middle East and North Africa. The right to levy taxes on their own communal institutions stopped, resulting in the closure of many.

During World War II, Turkey was officially neutral; however, life for all non-Muslims in Istanbul was made difficult, especially for the Jews. Already burdened with huge economic losses, the government levied an exorbitant amount of taxes on the Jewish community. Many were forced to sell or auction everything they owned.

When the State of Israel was established in 1948 thousands of Jews immediately left Istanbul for the new Jewish homeland. In the following years, a steady flow of Jews moved from Istanbul to Israel. Hence, only 20,000 Jews remain in the city, most of them engaged in commerce— particularly textiles— or are self-employed. A small number are lawyers, doctors, dentists, engineers, jewelers, architects and university professors. Some of the youth go into their family's businesses, while others attend the university. Generally, the wealthiest families send their children to college abroad.

The Jews of Istanbul are a close-knit group who are vigorously fighting the trend of assimilation in the Balkans. Subsequently, it is rare to have one or two intermarriages a year. The Jews take great pride in their community, which includes a high school, hospital, home for the elderly, thirteen Sephardic synagogues, one Ashkenazic and one Karaite. A daily minyan can be found in several synagogues even though most of the Jews do not live near them. On the island of Büyükada in the Sea of Marmara, wealthy Jews spend their summer holidays at a summer resort with its own synagogue. Here, children are brought to spend their summers in a Jewish atmosphere with the hope that friendships will result in marriage. Many of them do; another means of combating assimilation and intermarriage.

Istanbul, with sixteen functioning synagogues, has the largest and most stable Jewish community in the Balkans and prides itself on its strong Sephardic heritage. Neither assimilation or aliya will have much effect on the community in the coming years. Instead, its future lies in the hands of the precarious politics in the Middle East.

# IZMIR

*I*zmir, known as Smyrna before the establishment of the Turkish Republic, has had a Jewish settlement since the days of the Second Temple. When the first Sephardic exiles arrived, in the sixteenth century, they found a small Romaniot community comprised of descendants of Jews who had been slaves during the days of the Roman Empire.

In the seventeenth century, a significant and stable Jewish community began when Izmir became the leading Balkan commercial port. Jews moved to Izmir in large numbers, most of them Sephardic exiles from the Iberian peninsula. Though they brought few material possessions, they built on their self-assurance, strong will to survive and rich culture. These ingredients soon helped to create a Jewish golden age in the port city, similar to the one in Spain five hundred years previous. Yeshivot, Hebrew schools, synagogues and a printing press were soon established and the community became known for its physicians, merchants, industrialists, teachers, craftsmen and renowned rabbis.

In the midst of this growth and prosperity, on Tisha B'Av in 1626, Shabbatai Tzvi was born. According to the Jewish tradition, the Messiah would be born on this date when the majority of the Jews in the world were suffering. Steeped in the teachings of kabbalistic mysticism, Tzvi calculated that, in 1648, the Jews would be redeemed by the Messiah.

Shabbatai Tzvi convinced the Jews in Izmir that the significance of the two dates was not coincidental and that he was the Messiah. In order to gain the favor of the community, he precipitously annulled many of the religious Jewish laws that were rather bothersome. The leading rabbis immediately condemned him and forced him to leave the city. Initially, he traveled to Istanbul, then to Thessaloniki and other cities throughout the Balkan and Mediterranean areas. He traveled and preached for the next twenty years, attracting thousands of adherents. His influence shook the Jewish establishment throughout Europe in cities as far away as Avigon, Amsterdam, Venice and Vilna. In anticipation of the Messiah coming, many Jews liquidated their possessions in order to be able to afford the arduous trek to the Promised Land. Finally, in 1666, the Sultan, afraid that the movement might weaken his empire, arrested Tzvi. Faced with death or conversion to Islam, Tzvi chose Islam, much to the dismay of thousands of Jews across Europe. Some Jews followed Tzvi in converting to Islam and began wearing a turban, while still maintaining certain Jewish rituals. These apostates were known as Dönmehs (convert) and followed Tzvi to Thessaloniki and eventually Dulcigno, Albania, where he died in 1676. Today, in Izmir and a few other cities in Turkey, Dönmehs can still be found and are regarded as a Moslem sect.

The Jewish community in Izmir survived this calamity and continued to grow for the next two centuries. In 1868, it reached its greatest number at about 40,000, almost thirty percent of the city's population.

During the Russian-Japanese War of 1905 hundreds of Russian Jews found refuge in Izmir, effectively increasing the Ashkenazic community. However, in the years of the Balkan and First World War (1913–21), many Jews left Izmir for Greece, France and the United States due to the virulent form of nationalism under the leadership of Kemal Ataturk.

Another wave of emigration came during the 20s and 30s. Many of the eligible Sephardic men had immigrated during the war years to avoid the draft, while others sought better economic opportunities in South America. Consequently, the number of marriageable women outnumbered the single men by almost two to one. The women had heard and read—from many letters sent home—that there was plenty of land and Jews were creating their own autonomous agricultural colonies. Descriptions of the beautiful landscape and weather made South America seem a "Gan Aden" (Garden of Eden), so the women decided to follow the men.

During World War II, the Jewish population held steady at 15,000. Then, 10,000 immigrated to Israel in the years between 1948 and 1950. Since then, the community has continued to shrink. Today, most of the remaining 2,000 live in the new district of Alsancak. Previously, Karatas had served as the Jewish quarter for over four hundred years. The eight synagogues (six in the old souk market) still stand, representing some of the most ornate and unique interior decoration and architecture in the Balkans. Unfortunately, with the Jewish population diminishing around these synagogues, only three are open for prayers everyday. Four are closed and one is used only on Shabbat and holidays. The most attended and newest, "Shar Hashamayim," is in the Alsancak district, where Rabbi Nissim Barmaimon presides as the community's only spiritual leader, shokhet and mohel, as he has done for thirty years. Recently, however, a young man, Isak Alalouf, has returned home from studying to be a rabbi in Jerusalem and is helping his mentor to insure the community's religious and spiritual identity will continue—at least for several generations to come.

I had a conversation with Binyamin Avramento, the flamboyant secretary of the Jewish community. Through his words, one is able to sense how Jewish life once was—and is today—in Izmir:

"I grew up in a small village called Karsiyaka close to Izmir. There was a small Jewish community, enough to support one synagogue, where my brother and I had our Bar Mitzvahs. The synagogue has been closed for over twenty five years. Jewish life was nothing special to

speak of, everybody just kept to himself. But we did attend the synagogue as a community every evening for Minkhe and Maariv services. I remember my oldest brother's Bar Mitzvah which was in 1930. I was ten years old at the time. The whole family was there. Even my mother's side came all the way from Cairo. Unlike today, the celebration of the Bar Mitzvah began before Shabbat. It began that Thursday before early in the morning when my brother put on for the first time his new tefillin. On Shabbat he read the entire Torah portion, not just maftir (Hebrew: portion of Prophets read after reading the Torah). After the services, we had a big kiddush; everybody was invited. Then my brother got up and gave a discourse on the parsha (portion) he had read that morning—all in Hebrew! My brother had practiced with a well-known orator who spoke Hebrew fluently. Then, that evening, we had a large festive meal where we ate and sang Spanish songs until early in the morning. After witnessing my brother's Bar Mitzvah, I didn't want to have to wait three more years for mine. Especially since my father had given my brother a new bicycle. In 1930, having a new bicycle in our small village was a big deal—like have a new BMW motorcycle in Izmir today.

In 1937, we moved to Manisa, which is about fifty kilometers from Izmir. My father was the head of the post office there. There weren't any Jewish schools, so I went to a Turkish school. At that time there was a campaign in the country forcing all minorities to speak and learn in Turkish. But, despite these pressures from our government, we spoke Espagñol and French at home. The French came from my mother, who had lived in Cairo as a young woman.

Today, there are less and less Jews who speak Espagñol. Perhaps if we had a Jewish secondary school the youth would learn to speak it. We have a community center for the children twelve to eighteen years old. They have parties and dances there. The center is located downstairs from the "Shar Hashamayim." We tried to make a rule that made the youth come to the Friday evening services before they went to the club. We were trying to guarantee ourselves a minyan and teach the youth some religion and traditions. Some came, but not enough. We need this secondary school, like we had seventy years ago. The children's knowledge of Torah and Hebrew is becoming less and less. Without this sense of pride for one's past, present and future heritage, surely assimilation will swallow our Jewish community in twenty to thirty years. Even my son is married to a Moslem."

Istanbul: Rabbi Isak Haleva and his Bar Mitzvah student, Cem Bensason.

Istanbul: Marie Hodara, whose ancestors were from ancient Babylonia and not Spain, works at the Etz-Khayim synagogue.

Istanbul: Jak Peres, a retired fisherman, lives in the Kuzguncuk district, where, in the 1930s, 500 families resided. Only twenty remain.

Istanbul: Located in the Balat district, the Yambol synagogue was built over 400 years ago by Jews from Yambol, Bulgaria.

Istanbul: The Neve Shalom, the largest synagogue in the city, was the scene of a terrorist attack in 1986, during which twenty-one worshippers, including seven rabbis, were killed.

Istanbul: The Italian synagogue, also known as the Kal de los Frankos, is located in the Karaköy district.

Istanbul: Beit Israel synagogue is located in the newer Sisli residential district.

Izmir: The former Portuguese synagogue was built in 1907.

nbul: Built in 1842, the Merkaz synagogue serves
small Jewish community in Kuzguncuk on
baths and Jewish holidays.

Izmir: For lack of a
minyan, the Talmud
Torah-Khevra Kadishe
synagogue, built in
1900, has been closed
since 1987. ►

Istanbul: The former main sanctuary and Ark of the
Etz-Khayim synagogue in the Ortaköy district. In 1945,
memorial candles, left by the Shamash on the eve of Yom
Kippur, caused a fire which destroyed the synagogue.

◄ Izmir: The bima, or teva, as it is called by Sephardim in the Shalom synagogue. The shape of an ark suggests the boats that brought the Sephardim to the Ottoman lands.

Izmir: Built in the 16th Century, the Bikur Kholim synagogue has two daily morning services. ►

◄ Izmir: The Beit Israel synagogue, the largest in the city was built in 1917 and is located in the former Jewish Quarter, the Karatas District.

Izmir: A sign in Ladino in the in the La Senōra synagogue translates *It is prohibited to speak in the congregation."*

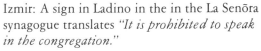

Istanbul: Interior of the Merkaz synagogue located in the Kuzguncuk district

Izmir: Binyamin Avramento is the secretary of the Jewish community.

Izmir: Yasef Lachana, originally from Adana, is the accountant for the Jewish community.

Istanbul: The entrance to the Etz-Khayim synagogue.

Istanbul: Israel Eskenazi, shamash of the Etz-Khayim synagogue, in his Shabbat uniform.

Istanbul: Nissim Levi, former gabai (treasurer) of Etz-Khayim, points to himself in a class photo of the Jewish Day School fifth grade of 1933, taken in front of the Etz-Khayim which burned in 1945.

Istanbul: Shamashim (pl.) Bayram (r.) and his friend standing in the Kuzguncuk synagogue courtyard.

Istanbul: Daniyel Baruh waits for afternoon services to begin in the Etz-Khayim synagogu

Istanbul: Reneta Seloni kisses the Holy Ark's curtains before leaving her Hebrew class.

Istanbul: Rabbi Pinto, originally from Edirne, completes a ketubah (Heb. marriage contract) at the Beit Din (Jewish court).

Istanbul: Rabbi Mose Benvenisti (r.) studies with Rabbi Rafael Pinto.

Izmir: A Jewish jeweler in the old souk district.

Istanbul: Nesim Licis (r.) has been one of Istanbul's nine kosher butchers since he was twelve years old.

Istanbul: The Kadoorie family, originally from Baghdad, founded the Laura Kadoorie Or-Khayim Jewish Hospital in 1930.

Istanbul: A pharmaceutical factory in the ...taköy district is a former Jewish orphanage.

Istanbul: Children running past a box factory, the former Jewish Day School.

The shamash Nissim Escafa, looking for the Torah portion to be r

the Fast day, the tenth of Tevet, in the La Senōra synagogue.

Istanbul: Yakov Meshulam has operated his kiosk in the Balat district for fifty-five years.

Istanbul: Strewn Jewish gravestones in the 400-year-old Ortaköy cemetery.

Izmir: Against a wall, gravestones of Jewish women who married Moslems are separated from other Jewish graves.

Istanbul: Isak Yarci pays respects to his mother's grave in the Ortaköy Jewish cemetery.

Izmir: Rabbi Leon J. Hakim, a businessman who offers his rabbinical services free to the community, says psalms for a deceased in the Jewish cemetery.

Izmir: The 1889 tombstone of a Jewish woman in the old Jewish cemetery.

Istanbul: The front entrance to the private Jewish Day School, which houses 425 students in grades k-11.

Istanbul: The kosher cafeteria at the Jewish Day School.

Izmir: Jewish students at recess at the Alliance Israélite Universelle Jewish Day School, which contains over 100 students in grades 1–5.

Istanbul: Viktor
Haim Beruhiel, a
chemical engineer
and cantor of
the synagogue,
teaches Hebrew
at Etz-Khayim.

Istanbul: Betina Seloni, shown sitting next
to her mother, attends Hebrew class every
Sunday at the Etz-Khayim synagogue.

Istanbul: The former Jewish quarters in the Balat district on the western side of the Golden Horn.

Istanbul: Looking across the Bosphorus to the Asiatic side.

# *Greece*

The history of the Jews in Greece begins after the destruction of the First Temple in Jerusalem in 586 B.C.E., when the Jews were sold into slavery and living on the Greek islands. Greek and Roman writers wrote about well-established Jewish settlements in the first century B.C.E. After the Jewish-Roman war (66–70 C.E.-Hasmonean uprising), the number of Jews on the Greek mainland and islands increased significantly as the victors sold more Jews into slavery. For eight centuries, under the Greeks and Romans, the Jews lived in relative peace outside of Palestine, so much so that the majority of the Jews adopted the language and customs of their rulers. This assimilation to Greek culture was known as Hellenization. Generally, the Jews forgot Hebrew, except for some liturgical prayers, and resorted to translating the Bible into Greek. This bible, known as the Septuagint, was written in Alexandria, Egypt, in the second and third centuries B.C.E. and was widely used. At that time, Alexandria was the largest Hellenist community in the Greek empire.

During the early and middle years of Byzantine rule, Jewish life became more difficult. After Constantine the Great converted to Christianity in 330 C.E., he and succeeding emperors periodically issued edicts which significantly limited the rights of the Jews. Until the twelfth century, despite repeated efforts to convert them, the Jews continued to prosper as physicians, artisans, weavers, dyers and farmers. The Greek Jews who were silk weavers and dyers were respected so highly that other European countries requested the use of their skills.

Life for the Jews grew increasingly richer when the Ottoman Turks began their conquest of the Balkans in 1365. During this time Jews from Hungary and the Iberian peninsula were fleeing from persecution and found refuge under the Turks in the north and central regions of Greece. With the final expulsion of the Sephardim from Spain and Portugal in the late fifteenth century, thousands of Jewish exiles found refuge in Turkish-ruled Greece. Soon, the Romaniot Jews, the highly acculturated Greek-speaking Jews, were completely assimilated by their Sephardic brethren. Except for a few Jewish-Greek speaking communities like Ioannina, Crete, Khalkis and Patras, the *lingua franca* for the Jews was Judeo-Spanish.

During the 471 years of Ottoman rule, Jewish life, culturally and religiously, grew to new heights. High point for the Jews was the appointment of Don Joseph Nasi (1524–79) as duke of the islands Naxos and Cyclade by Sultan Selim II in 1566. Born as a Marrano in Portugal, at the age of thirty he went to Constantinople, where he fully returned to Judaism by being circumcised. He befriended the Sultan's son Selim and soon rose to be minister of Naxos.

At the beginning of the nineteenth century, Thessaloniki became the leading Jewish commercial center and Rhodes became the leading center for Rabbinical scholars in the Balkans. Unfortunately, most of the wealth in Thessaloniki was in the hands of a few Jewish families. Most Jews eked out a living peddling and tinsmithing. The farther one traveled away from the sea towards the interior, the poorer the Jews became. This was especially evident in the provinces of Thessaly, Thrace and Macedonia. Until 1820, when Greece became independent of Turkey, the history of Greek Jewry was virtually identical to that of the Jews in Turkey.

Greece's independence brought drastic changes for the Jews, who suffered great human losses because of their years of loyalty to the

Turks. In Peloponnesus, some 5,000 Jews were killed, while the remainder sought refuge on the island of Corfu. Though the Jews were given their civic and political equality in 1821, further attacks and anti-Jewish riots caused many Jews to seek safe haven in Turkey, Egypt and Italy. Consequently, only 10,000 Jews remained in Greece at the beginning of the 20th century. In Thessaloniki (which remained under Turkish rule until 1912) there were some 90,000.

After World War I and the collapse of the Ottoman empire, the chaotic exchange of people between Turkey and Greece, particularly from the Anatolia and Aegean Sea areas, caused the Jewish population in Greece to swell to 100,000. The majority lived in the provinces of Macedonia (Thessaloniki) and Thrace. During the years of the Greek republic from 1924 to 1935, twenty four Jewish communities tried to cope with anti-Semitism and poverty. The restoration of the monarchy under Metaxas (1936–1941) was the end for Greek Jewry.

By June 2, 1941, Italy occupied part of Western Greece, Athens, Peloponnesus and Corfu. Bulgaria occupied western Thrace and Germany controlled Macedonia, eastern Thrace and the Greek islands, including Rhodes. At the time of the invasion, some 13,000 Jews fought in the Greek army.

In the beginning of the German occupation, the Jews of Thessaloniki faced eviction from their homes. They were taunted in the streets, arrested and randomly taken hostage to be ransomed at high sums. Formal edicts against Jews were enacted in July of 1942, when thousands of Jewish men were conscripted for forced labor. Soon afterwards, all Jewish property was confiscated or looted. In February of 1943, the Jews of Thrace and Macedonia were ordered to wear the yellow Star of David badges and were forced into ghettos. One month later, the Bulgarians and Germans began the deportation of these Jews and the Jews from the Greek islands to the concentration camps in Poland. The occupation of Greece resulted in eighty-nine percent of the Jewish community perishing during the war.

During the war, many Jews fought valiantly in the partisans, particularly in the province of Thessalia, where they controlled the mountains. Since many partisans were communists, after the war many Jews felt an allegiance to the party that had helped to save their lives. Consequently, during the Greek Civil War (December, 1944–February, 1945), many Jews fought on the side of the communists.

After World War II, the entire Jewish community was ravaged and destitute. Funds from the American Jewish Joint Distribution helped the survivors rebuild their lives and communities. In 1948, the Greek government set up an organization that dealt solely with the problem of compensation for the property lost by the Jews during the war. Much of the compensation came from the Greek and German governments and provided the much needed funds for the restoration of synagogues, the building of a new Jewish school and apartments for the elderly. By 1954, the majority of the work was completed.

Until recently, relations between Greece and Israel have been strained, although anti-Semitism has not been a large problem. The religious life of Greek Jewry never recovered from the war and today only a few synagogues have services during the holidays. Fewer have regular services on Shabbat.

When the Jewish youth who are living in the small towns reach college age, most go to universities in either Thessaloniki or Athens, thus depleting already small Jewish communities. Many youth are strong believers in Zionism and choose to spend a year in Israel studying, or even make aliya. A small resurgence has occurred among some of the Greek Jews in studying and maintaining certain aspects of Sephardic culture, particularly the cuisine and folk music. But the overwhelming feature is one of assimilation, which is causing a gradual decline in the number of Greek Jews, which presently totals 6,000.

# THESSALONIKI

Once the largest and most important Jewish community in Greece and the Balkans, Thessaloniki has existed for over two thousand years. Historical evidence points to a Jewish settlement having been established about 140 B.C.E. by Jews originally from Alexandria. In 50 B.C.E. the apostle Paul visited Thessaloniki and preached on three consecutive Sabbaths in the synagogue Etz Haim; which existed until 1917. According to Paul's own account, he did not find the community receptive to his new ideas.

During Byzantium rule, Thessaloniki was the second most important city in the empire. At that time, the Jews were known as Romaniots, had Greek names and spoke Greek as their first tongue, helping to create the city's extensive commercial ties with other ports throughout the Aegean region. Throughout the sixteenth century, they virtually monopolized the silk trade industry.

In 1169 Bejamin of Tudela visited and found an organized community of 5,000 Jews speaking Greek. Despite a certain degree of prosperity, however, the Jews were persecuted and suffered greatly. Tudela wrote: "The Jews are oppressed and live by silk-weaving."

The hostility Byzantine emperors felt towards their Jewish subjects that did not readily convert to Christianity continued through the Latin Empire created by the Crusaders (1204–1261), the despot rule of Theodore Angelus (1222–1230) and the seven year reign under the Venetians (1423–30).

Finally, in 1430, after the Turkish conquest, a new era began. Jews were allowed to openly practice Judaism and develop their community. The first wave of Jewish immigrants attracted to this liberal Ottoman policy was an Ashkenazic community from Hungary and Bavaria which established itself next to the existing Romaniot one and maintained its own cultural and religious ways into the twentieth century. Then, in the fifteenth and sixteenth centuries, Sephardim from Spain, Portugal, Italy, Sicily, France and North Africa settled in Thessaloniki, permanently changing the cultural landscape of the Jewish community. By 1553, 20,000 Jews resided in Thessaloniki; eighty percent were Sephardim. The number became so large that they were divided into thirty separate synagogues, each named after its hometown, such as Majorca, Lisbon, Toledo, etc. Each had its own communal institutions such as khevra kadishe (burials), gemilut khasidim (philanthropic), bikkur kholim (sick wards), bet din (court of law) and a yeshiva (Jewish school of higher learning).

In the sixteenth century, the yeshivot (pl.) maintained a high reputation for excellence, and rabbis and students from throughout Europe came to study and teach. Some of the outstanding scholars were Samuel Abrabanel, son of Isaac Abrabanel; Solomon Alkabez, author of the Sabbath hymn "Lekhah Dodi;" and Samuel diMedina, who wrote brilliant responses to rabbinic and khalakhic (Jewish law) treatises.

In addition to the rabbinical schools, the Jewish community supported secular institutions widely known for outstanding work in poetry, singing, medicine, natural sciences and astronomy. The Sephardic exiles had so assimilated the Romaniot — and some of the Ashkenazim — that they were speaking fluent Judeo-Spanish. The Sephardim's religiosity, scholarship and self-assurance had ushered in a "Golden Age." At this time, the poet Samuel Usque from Ferrara, Italy, coined the title "Thessaloniki, the Mother of Israel."

In the seventeenth century, the Jewish community suffered some disastrous fires and plagues, prompting a large number to leave. Nevertheless, in 1650, Jews numbered 30,000 —fifty percent of the total population. Thessaloniki continued as a prominent center of rabbinic and kabbalistic studies, attracting many Jewish personalities from throughout the Mediterranean. Probably the most enigmatic and influential was the self-proclaimed Messiah Shabbatai Tzvi. Expelled from his native Izmir, he arrived in Thessaloniki in 1657 and immediately began preaching in the synagogues, declaring himself as the Messiah. Shortly thereafter he was expelled by the leading rabbis of the city. Thirteen years later, a group of his followers called Dönmeh (Turkish-apostates) emulated him in converting to Islam and made Thessaloniki their center. After some years, they were forced to move to Turkey, where their descendants still reside primarily in Istanbul.

One positive result from the Shabbataian upheaval came in 1680 with the merging of the thirty independent congregations into one, led by a council of three rabbis so known for their honesty and fairness that Muslims and Greeks, who had cases involving Jews, preferred the Jewish courts to the Turkish.

In the eighteenth century the vast Ottoman Empire began to slowly disintegrate, adversely effecting the Jews of Thessaloniki economically. Much of the port's business was now under French and Italian merchants' control. Still, some Jews remained—like the descendants of the Portuguese conversos who had emigrated from Italy.

In the late eighteenth century, the Jewish population stood at 30,000.

The second half of the nineteenth century, westernization and secularization reached the city and Jewish community. A new port was built in 1889 and new technologies expanded industries. One family who took advantage of the expansive and prosperous times was the Allatinis. A very influential family, they possessed extremely successful textile mills. As a result of their success, they became very philanthropic with the Jewish community, aiding in the establishment of two modern Jewish schools in 1875, similar to that of the Alliance Israélite Universelle school founded in 1873. In 1883, the family built a ceramic factory and, three years later, they established Banquede Salonique, at its time the largest bank in the Balkans.

Thessaloniki continued to grow as trade with northern Europe became easier with the building in 1891 by Baron Maurice de Hirsch of the railway linking it with Skopje. Hirsch, another Jewish philanthropist, also had a noticeable influence on the Jewish community with the building, in 1891, of quarters for Jewish refugees from Russia. He also sponsored the Clara de Hirsch Hospital—named for his wife—in 1908. With ninety nine beds, it was the largest hospital in the city. Even the Zionist movement was heartily embraced by the community with the establishment of Khevrat Kadimah (The Forward Group) in 1899.

Between 1846 and 1939, the magnetism and intellectualism of the Sephardic community blossomed to such a degree that two-hundred-ninety-six journals and numerous newspapers were printed. Rabbi Yiouda Nehama published the first Ladino newspaper *El Lounar* (The Moon) in 1865. The journal *Salonik* (1869–70) was published as a multilingual paper in Ladino, Turkish, Greek and Bulgarian (Sofia). *La Solidaridad Ouvradera* (Workers Solidarity), a Socialist newspaper, began in 1911 and changed its name to *Avante* (Forward) during the Balkan Wars (1912–13). The Zionist group had several papers, including *La Esperanza* (The Hope) and *Lema 'am Yisrael* (Pro Israel). All in all, Judeo-Spanish was the lingua franca of the Jewish people—whether they were poor or rich, religious or secular.

Judeo-Spanish was so pervasive—especially in and among the neighborhoods and businesses along the docks—that most non-Jews working in the commercial district spoke it fluently. When Thessaloniki was captured in 1912 by the Greek army under the command of King

George of Greece, most Jews spoke Judeo-Spanish, Turkish and Arabic in that order — not Greek.

Thessaloniki was the most well-organized, tightly knit Jewish community in the Balkans. It was also the undisputed world capital of Sephardic culture up until the Holocaust. The community reached its zenith in size and religious and secular activities in 1908, with 90,000 Jews in a total population of 157,000.

Jewish influence was so strong that Thessaloniki's port closed on Shabbat and all gentile dockworkers took the day off. Jews worked in the maritime trade as shipbuilders, chandlers, harbor workers, sailors and ship pilots. Though they lived in all areas of the city, the majority lived primarily along the quays of the harbor. When Alexander Kyrland, a Norwegian author, visited the city in the early part of the century, he noted: "One could see hundreds of beautifully well-dressed Jews in their Sabbath best, or Oriental or Western style clothes, promenading along the seafront. And the non-Jews employed by the Jewish merchants could be seen strolling along too, enjoying this day of leisure."

The arrival of the Young Turk movement began the decline of the Jewish community. Some Jews (many socialists) supported the nationalistic fervor for a democratic Turkish republic because it was much more liberal than its Ottoman predecessor under the control of Sultan Abdul Hamid II. Other Jews were cautious of its real intentions. Consequently, many Jews began to leave Thessaloniki. Under the reign of the Young Turks, all minorities were granted equal status. For the Jews this meant losing some special privileges and having to serve in the Turkish army.

On August 19, 1917, a catastrophic fire in the center of Thessaloniki virtually destroyed the entire Jewish community, including thirty-four synagogues, community offices, ten yeshivot and eleven Jewish schools. 73,448 people were left homeless; 53,737 were Jewish. After the fire, the Greek government adopted a strict policy of hellenizing the city. Jews could not return to the burned out neighborhoods where they had lived. In 1922 the government inaugurated a law stating that all Salonikans had to refrain from working on Sundays, which meant Jewish businesses lost another day of trade. Many Jews left the city; a large number settled in Paris and Palestine.

After the forced relinquishment of the rest of Turkey's territorial holdings in Asia Minor (most of it to Greece), a mass of Greeks and Turks moved to their respective new republics. Approximately one-and-a-half-million Greeks moved to Greece, many to Thessaloniki. These Greeks, many of whom had never lived within the borders of the republic, felt a strong resentment towards the Jews, who were treated and lived relatively well under Ottoman rule. Jews in Thessaloniki, who spoke Judeo-Spanish and Turkish and little or no Greek, were looked upon as despised purveyors of Turkish culture. Consequently, anti-Semitism grew, resulting in several huge anti-Jewish riots, with loss of property and injuries among hundreds of Jews. The Greek Prime Minister Venizelos encouraged these provocative acts by adopting the slogan "Greece for Greeks," discounting the fact that Jews had lived in Greece for more than 2,000 years. Between the years of 1932 and 1933, 20,000 Jews left. But, despite the riots, fire and new city ordinances, the Jews proved their resilience by maintaining the high status the Sephardic community had held for over four hundred years.

On the eve of World War II, at 56,000, the Jewish community was still the largest in the Balkans, and maintained one of the most comprehensive European infrastructures. There were two Jewish choirs, a Maccabic sports club, various Zionist and Socialist organizations, Alliance schools — four trade and five community, four Rabbinical schools, over forty religious schools, thirty two large synagogues and sixty eight Beit Midrashim.

On April 9, 1941, the Germans marched into Thessaloniki and systematically began to quickly destroy the two-thousand-year-old Jewish community. On April 15, 1941, all members of the Jewish community council were arrested and its offices ransacked. Soon, placards forbidding Jews to enter cafes, libraries, concert halls and other public areas were posted around the city. On July 11, 1942, all Jewish males between the ages of eighteen and forty five were ordered to gather in the main square and stand at full attention under the hot boiling sun without any water for twelve hours. Several collapsed due to heat stroke and were immediately beaten senseless by the Nazis. Finally, at nightfall, the 10,000 men were sent to several work camps in the outlying areas, where they were forced to work in the hot sun for ten hours a day. Many died of malnutrition, heat stroke, exposure, malaria and beatings. Finally, after several months, the Germans agreed to exempt the Jews from the forced labor—in return for a ransom of over $100,000.00.

In December, 1942, the Germans made the Chief Rabbi of Greece, Rabbi Zvi Koretz (an Austrian by origin) the president of the new Jewish council. The Germans sent Rabbi Koretz to Germany, where he was subjected to intense propagandistic "brainwashing" for several months. Upon his return, he began preaching that, if the Jewish community totally complied with the Nazi authorities and appeased them with outward signs of respect for their authority, he, in turn, would be able to prevent deportation. In those tragic times—and still today—Rabbi Koretz is not remembered fondly by the few Jewish survivors of Thessaloniki.

Rabbi Halegua, the only rabbi in Thessaloniki today, recalls: "One day during the deportations I went to see the rabbi to see if there was any possible way we could help some Jewish families escape to the mountains which were held by the communist partisans. It was an afternoon of a rather cold early spring day. I had only a light top coat to wear as I had given my wool winter coat to my father. I came into his office in a rather rushed nervous manner and said, 'Your imminence, why do you tell the families that if they voluntarily go to the square they will be sent to Poland to live and work in much better conditions than we have here? Why do you take advantage of the others and myself?' Rabbi Koretz replied, 'But the Germans are taking advantage of me and I can have the Germans take you much sooner, don't talk to me!' As it happened, Rabbi Koretz died on the way to Bergen Belsen, while his wife and daughter managed to survive the war in Austria. After the war the Jewish community didn't condemn or pardon the rabbi. Only God can make that judgement."

From March 15, 1943 through August 7, 1943, nineteen convoys containing 45,000 Jews made the arduous trip to Poland. Those who survived the hellish trip were directly sent to Auschwitz, where the majority perished, while a few survived in Bergen Belsen. Others survived the forced labor camps, while some managed to escape to the mountains and seek refuge among the two communist partisan groups, ELLAS (Greek Popular Liberation Party) and EAM (National Liberation Front). The third partisan group fighting in the mountains was loyal to King Constantine and was not friendly towards Jews. After the war, only 2,000 Jews returned to Thessaloniki.

Today, the Jewish community numbers somewhere between 800 and 1,000. There are two synagogues, the Yad Le Zikaron and the Monastiriot. The Yad Le Zikaron was built in the 1920s by a wealthy merchant so that neighborhood merchants would have a place to worship during the day. The previous synagogue had been destroyed by fire in 1917. Today, it has services three times a day every day of the week, except on Sundays. The Monastiriot was erected in 1925 by Jewish families from Monastir (Bitolj), Yugoslavia. It has survived because it was used by the Red Cross as a warehouse during the war. Today, services are only held on High Holidays.

The offices of the Jewish Community Center share a building with the Jewish Club. Youth gather several times during the week to relax, play games, watch videos and celebrate Jewish holidays. The Jewish School, which opened in 1980, occupies a building built in 1902 and originally called Matalon Levyonim (Hebrew: charity for the poor). Poor Jews were able to receive free food for the Jewish holidays while their children received a hot lunch every day.

After the meal, the children stayed and participated in several different sports and youth activities organized by the local Maccabi Sports Union. Today, it has eighty students in the first through sixth grades.

Thessaloniki was once known as "The Mother of Israel." Sadly, the Jewish community's former glories are mostly found in archives of aging photographs and the fading memories of elderly survivors.

# LARISSA

Larissa, the biggest city in the province of Thessalia, has the largest and most active Jewish community. A small group of Turkish Sephardic Jews established a community in the mid-sixteenth century and, from that time through the nineteenth century, the growth and prosperity of the city was closely connected to that of Volos, a port city on the Aegean Sea. The Jews had set up close commercial ties with Volos insuring that their goods would be brought to Larissa to be sold or traded throughout Asia Minor.

In the beginning of the twentieth century there were 600 Jews in Larissa. After the Balkan Wars (1912–13), the community grew by taking in Jewish refugees from the war-torn Greek islands. In 1940, the community reached 1,175.

When the war began between Italy and Greece, Jews fought and died in the Greek army. When the Italians defeated the Greeks, they occupied Thessalia. Immediately, anti-Jewish restrictions on bank accounts and a curfew were imposed, but, for the most part, life continued in much the same pattern as before until the Germans arrived.

Most Jews in Larissa had luckily heeded warnings they had heard from Jews who had managed to escape from Thessaloniki and join the partisans. When the Germans took power from the Italians in 1943 nearly eighty percent of the Jewish community had already fled to the mountains. The mountains were partisan strongholds, providing safety, comfort and food for those Jews who managed to reach them. More importantly, they provided an eternal hope for the nation that Greece would one day be free again.

One morning while visiting the Jewish community office, I met Mr. Alberto Albelansis, a native of Larissa and a retired textile merchant. He told me how he and his family survived the German occupation:

"My family and I escaped to a village in the mountains about thirty kilometers from Larissa. This was in 1941 during the Italian occupation. We came back in the spring of 1943 because we had heard a rumor that the city was being liberated by the English and the Italians were being driven out. The Italians did capitulate, but the English were nowhere to be found and the Germans were quickly advancing towards Larissa from Thessaloniki. We escaped one more time to the mountains and stayed until the Germans were defeated in October of 1944. Most of the Greek Jews who survived in Greece, like ourselves, owe their lives to the partisans."

Regrettably, not all Jews heeded the warnings or were able to escape the Nazi hordes. Those captured were either shot for aiding the partisans or sent directly to Aushwitz or Birkenau. One of the few deportees to have survived and returned to Larissa after the war, Mrs. Duka Moisses, hosted a WIZO (Women's International Zionist Organization) meeting which I was invited to attend.

In March 1944, Mrs. Moisses, along with all seven members of her immediate family, were in hiding just outside the city, but were told by a Jewish collaborator paid by the Germans that it was safe to come and receive food if they would just register with the German authorities. They were seized immediately after they arrived in Larissa. They were held under armed guard in a freezing warehouse while the Germans lured more cold and starving Jews to leave the mountains and villages with false promises of food and warmth. In three days, the Germans had rounded up 425 Jews. In one week, they were deported to Birkenau. Duka Moisses was one of thirty four to survive, the only one of her family. When she returned after the war, she found that a few of her relatives had survived in the mountains.

Today, 500 Jews remain in Larissa. The close-knit community's spiritual leader, Rabbi Eliahu Sabetai, originally came from Athens. He studied for the rabbinate in England and came to Larissa in 1986, the first rabbi in twenty-five years. He is also a shokhet and administers the koshering on the Jewish holidays for Thessaloniki, Volos and Trikala as well. The community has a Day School attended by every Jewish youth. Although it has only fifteen students this year it has a noted reputation for high scholarly achievement, as well as having the best Hebrew language program in Greece. Hebrew and Jewish studies are taught by Mr. Iacov Filoys, who studied in Jerusalem and returned to Larissa to become a merchant. He has been a beloved Hebrew teacher for thirty-two years and, under his guidance, the Day School and Jewish youth club have remained active on a national level in spite of a diminishing student population.

Every year, a large Jewish symposium is sponsored throughout Greece in a designated city. These gatherings are for making new friendships and rekindling old ones, as well as for conducting scholarly lectures. Last year, Larissa sponsored one of the most successful.

The community's fervor for Jewish scholastics can be measured by the number of Larissa boys who went on to study for the rabbinate: Chief Rabbi Arrar and Rabbi Mizan of Athens, one who studied and is now a chemist in Holland, another who studied and is a doctor in Italy, a rabbi in Paris and a rabbi in Israel.

During the summer months, many Jewish youth spend their vacations at the Jewish camp Litókhóro, located halfway between Thessaloniki and Larissa on the seaside. Their special bonds they maintain with their city and Jewish community continue when they attend university. Generally, they are among the more active members in their Jewish youth groups and often visit among their families during the holidays. With the opening of a new university in Larissa in 1991, more Jewish youth are expected to remain and study at home and settle in Larissa after they finish school.

During my three month trek, Larissa was one of the most hospitable and warm Sephardic communities I visited.

# VOLOS

In the mid-sixteenth century, a significant Jewish community began in Volos when Sephardim exiled from the Iberian peninsula settled in the port city. They soon established commercial trade ties with their brethren in other ports along the Aegean coast.

Though some Ashkenazim from Hungary and Bavaria also settled in Volos, the Sephardim have remained an overwhelming majority. Unlike other Balkan Sephardic communities, it has never had a separate Ashkenazic synagogue, consequently, the *lingua franca* among all Jews has been Judeo-Spanish.

At the turn of the century, the community reached 1,500. During the ensuing Balkan and First World War, their numbers began to decline, with Jews immigrating to Athens, Egypt, France and the United States.

During the years between the World Wars, the Jewish community was small, but active. Their spiritual leader was Rabbi Moisses Simeon Pesakh (1869–1955), who was born in Larissa and educated in Thessaloniki. He became Chief Rabbi of Volos in 1898. There were two cantors, a Jewish school with grades one to six, a Maccabi sports club called Ha-Koakh (The Strong) and a Maccabi self-defense club.

Seventy one Volos Jews fought in the Greek army at the beginning of the Greek and Italian War in 1940. During the war, the Jewish community was able to maintain an air of normalcy and kept most of the Jewish institutions functioning, despite the pro-Nazi leaning of Johannes Metaxas' Greek government. During the later Italian occupation, some nine hundred Jews, most of them financially secure, managed to escape from the city. In the northern provinces of Thrace, Macedonia and particularly Thessaloniki, the situation was much worse under the Germans and the Bulgarians. Some of the Jews who managed to escape from those areas came to Volos and found temporary refuge.

On September 8, 1943, when the Italians capitulated to the Allies, the Germans took complete control of the province of Thessalia, which included Volos. Immediately, Rabbi Pesakh was brought to the offices of the German high command. He was commanded to produce a list containing the names and addresses of all the Jews in the city, under the pretext that the Germans needed to keep track of where food rations were to be given and how much according to the size of the family. Rabbi Pesakh knew differently and asked to be given three days to complete the task. He then went directly to the mayor, asking him to rally the townspeople to support the escape of Jews to the mountains or safe houses in the countryside. Three days later, he returned to the Germans asking for more time to complete the list. During the next two weeks, with the Rabbi dangerously stalling the Germans, the church and townspeople aided most of the Jews in fleeing the city.

Although the Germans were informed by a few unscrupulous Greeks that most of the Jews were fleeing, they preferred to look the other way. Two weeks later, some thirty Jews returned because they could not stand the cold and lack of food. They had also heard rumors that the Germans would not deport them. Rabbi Pesakh then put up flyers with his signature, verifying that the Germans were to begin deportations to Poland the next week and that any Jew remaining in Volos was endangering himself. Livid, the Germans offered a large monetary reward to anyone who would give them information leading to Rabbi Pesakh's arrest.

On October 1, 1943, Rabbi Pesakh, at the age of seventy four, with the aid of the local communist youth partisans, escaped by donkey to the mountains. He remained there for the duration of the war. His work in Volos did not stop. Before he left, he had managed to obtain an illegal two-way radio. With it, the partisans were able to communicate with each other over long distances at a time when sending messages was extremely difficult and dangerous in the rocky terrain.

On March 2, 1944, 135 Volos Jews were sent to the extermination camp Birkenau. Only five returned. Rabbi Pesakh survived, but his wife died from stress and disease and his daughter was killed on her escape to a farm house. After fourteen months of German occupation, seven hundred Jews returned to Volos, most from the mountains and nearby villages. A few returned from the labor camps in Germany.

With monetary aid from the Joint Distribution Committee and from individual Jews abroad, these survivors rebuilt the Jewish community in Volos, with a new synagogue, ORT trade school and Old Age Home.

Though Rabbi Pesakh was aging, he continued to be a leader and pillar of great respect, working tirelessly for the good of all Volos, until his death in 1955. At his funeral, he was mourned by the entire city and received exalted eulogies from the mayor, the church and many Jews who owed their lives to him.

The Jewish community was again devastated and had to be rebuilt when a severe earthquake struck in November of 1955. In the years since, the community has decreased in size as many Jews immigrated to Israel and others, after attending universities in Athens or Thessaloniki, did not return to Volos.

Today, there are 150 Jews without a rabbi. Every Saturday after Shabbat services, a group of five or six children learn Hebrew and Jewish history and customs from their teacher, Mr. Halegri Francess, who travels from Thessaloniki. When there is a Bar Mitzvah, Rabbi Sabatai from Larissa comes to Volos to help conduct the prayers and Torah reading.

Because Volos is a short train ride from Larissa (many people commute for work), the Jews have a special relationship with their brethren there, often looking to them for both financial and cultural support. When I visited Volos, arriving by train from Larissa, I met Mr. Ilias Kones, the vice-president of the Jewish community, who generously showed me around. Upon seeing the smallness of the Jewish community, I was struck by the close comradery and high esteem the members showed for each other and their guests. After the Friday night kiddush, during which there was plenty of food, drink and bantering from young children, Mr. Kones took me to his office and showed me three black and white photographs of the synagogues that had existed in Volos in this century. His poignant comment was:

"The Germans destroyed this one and those of us who survived rebuilt it. The earthquake destroyed this one eleven years later—God's will. And those of us who remained rebuilt the synagogue again. And today you prayed in this small but beautiful synagogue. We are a small kehille (Jewish community), but my grandchildren I'm sure will be here to make a kiddush for your children when they come to visit us."

# TRIKALA

Remains from an ancient synagogue attest to the antiquity of Trikala's Jewish community, which remained small until the arrival of Hungarian, Spanish and Sicilian refugees in the sixteenth century. The Sephardim introduced wool weaving which became a lucrative trade, doing so well that Sephardic refugees from throughout the Ottoman Empire began to emigrate to the small city. Eventually, they became the majority and assimilated the Ashkenazim to their ways and culture.

As in Larissa, the Pinios river runs through Trikala to the Aegean Sea and served as a trade artery. Goods were shipped downstream to moored vessels which carried the products to ports throughout Asia Minor. Other times merchants shipped their products to Larissa, then overland to Volos from which they were traded with ports in the south Aegean Sea.

These commercial ties — and the fact that Trikala, Larissa and Volos were the three main Jewish communities in Thessalia province — have kept the cities in close contact through the years.

At the turn of the century the Jewish community numbered 800. But, because of economic and political occurrences during the Balkan and World War I, the number had declined to 550 just prior to World War II. Nevertheless, it still supported two synagogues and two rabbis.

During the Nazi occupation, many Jews escaped and found refuge in the nearly villages and mountains controlled by the partisans. Those who did not heed the warnings they received from Thessaloniki were caught and deported to the extermination camps in Poland.

Mr. Israel Yitzkhak Kapeta was born in Trikala and was a carpenter before he retired. Now the community's shamash (beadle), he told me of the fateful circumstances which engulfed he and his family during the war:

"I had been told by our Greek neighbors that the Germans were in the main square and beginning to search from house to house for Jews. I immediately left for the mountains, as I couldn't get back to my house to warn my family. The only street that led from my neighborhood to my house was filled with fascists. By going immediately to the mountains I hoped to get some guns from the communists (partisans) and shoot my family free if need be. My mother, brother, two uncles, two aunts and one cousin were trapped on the side of the town where the Germans were marching and driving towards. My mother, seeing the situation, immediately and quietly began waving with her hands in an animated motion showing the family the escape route that led to the mountains through some back alleys that few people knew about. Finally, a German soldier came to our family's house where a Greek neighbor of ours was standing on the porch. The German barked, 'Where are the dirty Jews? Are they inside? Speak up now!' Our neighbor — a tall, slender, clean-shaven man with light brown hair — pretended not to understand and said, in Greek, 'I am the only Jew here. . .the only one!' Again, the German barked out his question and again, trying to be as convincing as possible, our neighbor repeated his answer. Of course, the German ass didn't understand Greek. Getting angrier, he pushed my neighbor to the ground, went into the house, ransacked the place, but found no Jews, and left in a great rage. While this was all going on, my mother was leading our family to the mountains. When she saw me, she was overwhelmed with joy. She thought I had been captured by the Germans. We stayed in the mountains for the duration of the war, always on the go, concerning ourselves only with our safety and finding food."

Today, there is one synagogue serving the community's sixty Jews. There is no rabbi. For the High Holidays, the community employs a rabbi who comes from Istanbul. For the other holidays, Cantor Moisses Gannis leads the services. When there is a young boy who will have his Bar Mitzvah, he goes to Larissa and studies with Rabbi Sabatai. Next to the synagogue in the courtyard is a small building that serves as a social hall where Wizo meetings are held and Kabbalat Shabbat, Purim and other festivals are celebrated.

With only ten Jewish children—most from mixed marriages—the future of the Jewish community in Trikala does not look to be a long and prosperous one.

# KHALKIS

Jewish existence in Khalkis dates from 200 B.C.E. when Jews were taken as slaves to the island of Evvoia, off the eastern coast of Greece, by the Phoenicians. The Jewish community in Khalkis is believed to be the oldest in continuous existence in Greece. The name of the city itself had Jewish origins, coming from the Hebrew word khalek, which means "crushed stones" or "pebbles," an appropriate name since most of the land was rocky and strewn with countless stones.

When Alexander the Great conquered the Persians, the living standards for the Jews began to improve as they became involved in several trades, including weaving, farming and working as sailors.

The Jews adapted so well to Greek culture that many forgot how to read, write or speak Hebrew, and even left Judaism altogether. When Benjamin of Tudela visited Khalkis, he recorded in his memoirs that there were 2,000 Jews, of which 95% were completely assimilated and undistinguishable from their Greek neighbors, while the other 5% were very religious scholars.

In 1258, the Venetians conquered Khalkis and immediately oppressed the Jewish community with numerous edicts and heavy taxes. Not until 1458 did they relax their grip and allow them religious and economic autonomy, primarily so that they could benefit from the Jewish mercantile contacts with other ports throughout the Aegean Sea.

During the fourteenth century, the Jewish community came under several different attacks from pirates. Each time, their homes, shops and synagogue were plundered, while the women were raped. Finally, in 1470, the Ottoman Turks defeated the Greeks in a battle which completely destroyed the city and decimated its population. The Turks, however, provided the Jewish community protection from the marauding pirates and the Jews began to rebuild their destroyed community.

Word soon spread that Khalkis Jewish life under the Ottomans was flourishing. Unlike other Jewish communities in the Aegean Sea region, Khalkis remained overwhelmingly Greek-Romaniot and not Sephardic. The Sephardic culture never took root and became noticeable only after the Balkan War and World War I. Then, the few Sephardim who had been living on islands near the Turkish coast emigrated to Khalkis.

In 1833, Greece once again ruled the island of Evvoia. By 1840, between 350 to 400 Jews comprised part of Khalkis' 4,000 inhabitants. Although the relationship was generally friendly, attacks on the Jewish community continued. During a procession held by the church on the Christian Good Friday holiday, participants and admirers stoned Jewish houses and looted Jewish shops. This anti-Semitic practice occurred every year until 1935, when Prime Minister Eliftherios Venizelos came to power and put a stop to the practice.

In 1894 much of the community was destroyed in a devastating earthquake. Jews from Europe and the United States quickly responded with financial contributions, and Baron Ferdinand Rothschild personally visited the destroyed community. Distressed that the wall enclosing the Jewish cemetery had been destroyed and farmers and townspeople were using the headstones to rebuild their homes and the wall surrounding the castle, he donated money to rebuild it.

On the eve of World War II, the Jewish population of Khalkis numbered 400, a small, but active, community with a synagogue (rebuilt in 1855), a Jewish school, a Maccabi sport club and many Jewish owned shops.

During the war, most of the Jewish community found refuge in Athens and with the communist partisans in the mountains. Some Jews remained on the island, hidden by priests. The community's books and Torah were also hidden in several churches and returned after the war. The first senior Greek officer to die in battle was a Jewish colonel, Mordecai Frizis, from Khalkis, killed in a battle against the Italians in Albania.

Many Jews did not return to Khalkis after the war and economic recovery was much slower than on the Greek mainland.

Today, about eighty Jews reside in the ancient city. The leader is Mr. Mario Massis, who was born in Khalkis and owns a department store. In his spare time, he is writing a history of the Jewish community and has begun to restore the only two remaining Jewish sites: the synagogue and the cemetery. The synagogue has been carefully refurbished in its mid-nineteenth century tradition, while the cemetery is being literally restored stone by stone. Some gravestones have been found dating as far back as 1,200 years. Mr. Massis's wife, Zermain, is active in the local WIZO chapter, which meets weekly to discuss matters concerning themselves and international events. They also help plan and prepare for the Jewish holidays and festivals.

Since the community is small, all Jewish holidays are celebrated communally. When a boy begins to prepare for his Bar Mitzvah, he must travel to Athens to study with Rabbi Mizan; however, the Bar Mitzvah takes place in the Khalkis synagogue.

Though Khalkis is only a ninety minute ride from Athens, many youth are leaving the community after they graduate high school or college. Better economic opportunities and a more cosmopolitan lifestyle beckon them to the mainland.

Sadly, the last chapter of the 2,500 year old history of the Jews of Khalkis has begun to be written.

# ATHENS

Up until the Balkan War (1912–13), the Athens Jewish community played a minor role, especially compared to Thessaloniki and Rhodes. However, the Athens community was an ancient one, established during the conquest of Palestine by Alexander the Great. Some historians believe that Jews were brought to Athens and the nearby islands as slaves. Archaeological evidence from the island of Aegina indicates a Jewish community during the time of Alexander the Great, when the wealthy community of Alexandria had built a lavish synagogue on the island.

The first concrete information on the Jews of Athens exists in the writings of St. Paul from his journey throughout the Mediterranean in 45–57 A.D. While preaching to both Jews and gentiles at the synagogue in Athens, St. Paul noted how many gentiles in the audience were enamored of Judaism. A sense of Jewish life can also be found in the writings of Benjamin of Tudela, who described Mediterranean and Near East Jewish life in the cities and villages he visited during the years 1165–1173: "The Greeks hate the Jews, good and bad alike, and beat them in the street...Yet the Jews are rich and good, kindly and charitable, and bear their lot with cheerfulness."

Even after the Turkish conquest by Muhammad II in 1456, few Jewish families inhabited the city. After the expulsion of the Jews from Spain in 1492, a few families found refuge in Athens, but their total numbers barely reached 100 in the early nineteenth century.

During the Greek revolution (1821–29) against the Ottoman Empire, the Jewish community was destroyed. When the Greek state was established, a new community was developed by Jewish settlers from Bavaria who accompanied King Otto I. Initially representatives of European firms trying to establish themselves in the new Greek capital, they were followed by a wave of Sephardim from Izmir and Rhodes, along with Romaniot Jews from the ancient community of Khalkis. The fledgling community had no rabbi or synagogue and was under the protection of the French Duchess Sophie de Plaissance.

The community of 200 was officially recognized in 1889 and, in 1904, erected a new synagogue, the first new one in several hundred years. Attracted by a flourishing financial and social climate, more Jews moved to Athens after the Balkan Wars and another spurt of growth came after the terrible fire in Thessaloniki in 1917 which destroyed 70% of the Jewish community. After World War I and the fall of the Ottoman Empire, they were joined by hundreds of Greek Jews leaving Asia Minor.

In October 1940, Italy invaded Greece, but, with the help of British reinforcements, the Greek army forced the Italians back into Albania. When the Germans successfully invaded Greece in the early spring of 1941, they divided the country into three zones: German, Bulgarian and Italian. In the summer of 1942, the Germans began rounding up Thessaloniki Jews for forced labor and eventual deportation. Some 3,000 of them managed to escape to Athens, which was under a more lenient Italian rule. When the Italians capitulated to the Allies in September 1943, the Nazis immediately took over their zone under the command of SS General Jurgen Stroop. Stroop had recently led the destruction of the Warsaw ghetto and the Thessaloniki deportation. On October 7, 1943, he published a decree ordering all Jews to register at the synagogue within forty eight hours. Many, on the insistence of the Chief Rabbi Elijah Barzilai, had already heeded the warnings from Thessaloniki and either fled the city to the partisan held mountains or sought safe houses in the city limits owned by gentiles. In addition to those who escaped, a large majority survived because of the local populace, the Orthodox Church and the farsightedness of the Chief Rabbi, who destroyed the registry of all the names and address of the city's Jews. Unfortunately, some Jews were found with the aid of unscrupulous Greeks.

On the Sabbath evening of March 24, 1944, however, eight hundred Jews were captured near the synagogue and were immediately sent to Auschwitz. Five days later, a similar convoy of Jews from Athens and the surrounding area followed.

After the liberation, 5,000 Jews emerged from hiding; 1,500 immigrated to Israel. In 1945, the Joint Distribution Committee began to rehabilitate the survivors and the community. Slowly, they began to rebuild their infrastructure, including a new synagogue in 1947. The synagogue that existed before the war was small and had been partially destroyed by the Germans,

who used it as a warehouse. Today, the original synagogue is part of the Jewish community's offices.

Through the years, the Jews have numbered between 3,000 and 3,500, slightly less than half the current Greek population. They enjoy a full array of organizations, institutions and activities: WIZO, Aviv, B'nai and B'not B'rith chapters, a Zionist Union group, a Jewish Day School handling kindergarten to sixth grade, a Community Center with a kosher restaurant, a monthly magazine *Chronika* and a Maccabi Sports Club.

Though the community is close knit, intermarriage and immigration to Israel is threatening its future existence. This quote from a Jewish shop owner I met while exploring the neighborhood around the synagogue sums up its fate succinctly: "The Athenian Jewish community's history has a long resilient past, but its future will be a short one for those writing about it in a few generations to come."

Athens: Lydia Eshkenazi is the head of the Greek JDC, for which she has worked since 1945.

Athens: Established with funds from the American Jewish Joint Distribution Committee in 1960, the Jewish Day School is located in the affluent suburb of Psychico.

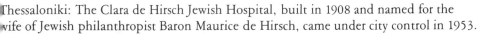

Thessaloniki: The Clara de Hirsch Jewish Hospital, built in 1908 and named for the wife of Jewish philanthropist Baron Maurice de Hirsch, came under city control in 1953.

Athens: A former synagogue, the Jewish Community Office was used as a warehouse by the Nazis. After the war, it was a shelter for concentration camp survivors.

Trikala: Esther Kapeta, originally from Larissa, in her home.

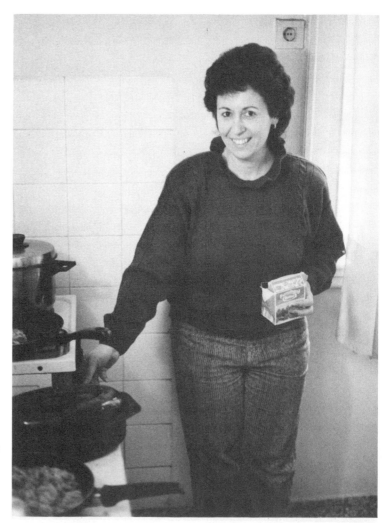

Thessaloniki: Rena Molho is an expert on the history of the Jews in the region.

Trikala: Yisrael Itzhak Kapeta, a retired carpenter, holds a photo of his parents, Itzhak and Sara.

Thessaloniki: Rabbi Moshe Itshak Halegua reads from the Torah.

Thessaloniki: Mois Eshkenazi is the shamash of the Yad L'Zikaron synagogue.

Thessaloniki: Yosef Tarabolo
practices his Torah portion
for his Bar Mitzvah.

Volos: Evening Shabbat services.

Larissa: Ten year old Alberto Begas waits for Friday night services to begin.

Athens: Putting on tefillin (Heb. phylacteries) before morning services.

Athens: Rabbi Mizan (r.) is the Jewish community's mohel and shokhet.

Volos: Ilias Kones leads the Shabbat kiddush.

Athens: The Beth Shalom synagogue was built in 1947.

Thessaloniki: The congregation of the Monastiriot synagogue originally came from Monastir, Yugoslavia. Three of nineteen survived Nazi occupation.

Trikala: The synagogue courtyard.

Trikala: The synagogue
and community center.

Khalkis: The synagogue, built in 1849, stands on the original foundation of one erected in the 17th century.

Trikala: Eli Kabelis, secretary of the Jewish community, standing next to the Holy Ark.

Thessaloniki: The interior of the Monastiriot synagogue.

Volos: Interior of the synagogue, originally built in 1870.

Larissa: Interior of the Etz Khayim synagogue, built in the 17th century.

Khalkis: Interior
of the synagogue.

Larissa: A memorial structure to the 235 local Jews who died in the Holocaust. The graffiti written in chalk is anti-Semitic.

Volos: A memorial to Volos Jews killed in the Holocaust.

Thessaloniki: A memorial to the 56,000 local Jews who were murdered in Auschwitz.

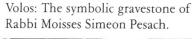

Volos: The symbolic gravestone of Rabbi Moisses Simeon Pesach.

Thessaloniki: A square and apartment complex originally owned by the Jewish community. The sign reads *The Square of the Jewish Martyrs.*

Larissa: The anti-Semitic *"Jewish pigs turn into soap"* on the door to the synagogue courtyard is answered by *"Nazi, pigs-traitors."*

Thessaloniki: Women come to the Jewish club to socialize and play cards.

Camelia Begas, secretary of the Jewish community, kneels on the floor during a meeting of the local chapter of WIZO (Women's International Zionist Organization), held at the home of Duka Moisses.

Larissa: Celebrating an Oneg Shabbat at the Jewish Club.

Larissa: Hebrew teacher Iacov Filoys and some of his former
students pose in front of the Jewish Day School.

Larissa: A Greek butcher carries kosher meat, but only during Jewish holidays.

hessaloniki: The Jewish Day School, which opened in 1980, occupies a 1902
uilding originally called Matalon Leyonim (Heb. charity for the poor).

Thessaloniki: The Molho Book Store,
established in 1888 by Meir Molho and
presently operated by his grandson Joseph,
is the oldest in the city and one of the
oldest in the country.

Thessaloniki:
The caretaker
of the Jewish
cemetery located
in the suburb of
Stayrouplis.

Athens: The closed
Jewish cemetery.

◄ Khalkis: Over the years, the ancient cemetery containing
1,200 year old graves has often been desecrated by vandals.

Larissa: Two signs on a tree inside the Jewish
cemetery perpetuate the custom of giving a
small donation for its upkeep. The Greek sign
reads *"Give whatever you have;"* the Hebrew
reads *"cash box."*

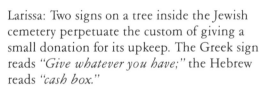

Khalkis: An old Jewish
gravestone, dating
from 1745.

Volos: The Jewish cemetery.

Larissa: Iacov Filoys teaching Hebrew to his students.

Athens: Once a week, Ziva Bracha, an Israeli, teaches Hebrew to Jews and non-Jews at the Jewish club.

Larissa: Recess time at the Day School.

Thessaloniki: Mano Bienvenida is the lady shamash of the Monastiriot synagogue. Her late husband Avram had been the shamash for forty years.

Khalkis: Mario and Zermain Maissis, leaders of the Jewish community, in their home.

Larissa: Alberto Albelansis, in the Jewish community's office.

Thessaloniki: A resident of the
Saul Modiano Jewish Old Age
Home built in 1980. Supported by
the Jewish community, the home
is able to house sixty five residents.

Larissa: A member of the Jewish community out for a walk on Shabbat afternoon.

# *Portugal*

There are references to Jews living in Portugal as early as 900 C.E., when the country was under Arab domination. When the first Christian king, Alfonso I (1139–85) was crowned, synagogues already existed in Lisbon, Santarem, Oporto (Porto) and Beja. It was not until Alfonso III (1248–79), however, that a distinct Portuguese communal life emerged.

Alfonso III recognized the Jews as having a separate community. He appointed a Chief Rabbi, who, in turn, named seven judges, one for each regional center. These dayyanim (Hebrew judges), with their staffs, had full authority to settle all civil and criminal cases involving Jews. All decisions could be appealed before the Chief Rabbi and his executive staff. This semi-autonomous rule was the first of its kind in Europe. Jews enjoyed it until the creation of the Vaad Arba Aratzot (Council of the Four Lands) in Poland (1592–1764).

The Jews prospered. By the fifteenth century, they had contributed greatly. As Portugal became a world power economically, militarily and cul-

turally, they achieved prominence as court physicians, printers, astronomers and treasurers. Some of the more notable were Judah Abravanel, the royal treasurer; his son, Isaac, a scholar and famous Bible commentator; and Abraham Zacuto, the most famous Portuguese astronomer. Even the exploration of Vasco da Gama, whose discovery of the sea route to India ushered in the expansion of Portugal, was greatly aided by the use of Jewish financing, map makers and ship-instrument manufacturers.

The Jews' successes, however, were accompanied by anti-Semitic outbreaks conspired and initiated by the Catholic clergy. During the reign of Alfonso V (1325–57), the Jews were forced to pay an inordinate amount of taxes, had difficulties in emigrating and were forced to wear yellow badges that identified the wearers as Jews. In 1350, the church accused the Jews of spreading the Black Plague throughout Portugal and incited the populace to attack them wherever they lived.

With the expulsion of the Jews from Spain in

1492, some 150,000 fled to Portugal, but only enormous bribes to King John II (1481–95) allowed the wealthiest families, artisans and craftsmen to stay. Some 100,000 paid a smaller head tax and were permitted to remain only eight months. After that time they were forced to board unseaworthy ships for destinations unknown. Most perished at sea. A few landed in Morocco. Today, there are a number of Moroccan Jews who trace their ancestry back to those fortunate few.

With the betrothal of Emanuel I to the daughter of King Ferdinand and Queen Isabella, the end for the remaining Portuguese Jews was at hand. Emanuel wanted to keep the Jews, hoping to retain the advantages of their diligence, business acumen and scholarship, but, pressured by his in-laws, he decreed on December 4, 1496 the exile of all Jews and Moslems from Portugal. Three months later, Emanuel banned all emigration and forcibly baptized thousands of Jews. These converts were known as New Christians, Conversos or Marranos (Spanish swine) and were portrayed as religious Christians. Within their homes and hearts they privately remained Jewish. Despite the forced baptisms, the general Portuguese populace still regarded these new converts as Jews and continually harassed them. In 1506, some two thousand New Christians were killed in a pogrom in Lisbon. The church felt that the New Christians, however faithful they outwardly seemed to Catholicism, could not be trusted and, through intermarriage, would inevitably cause *limpieza de mala sangre* (impurity of the blood). The church believed that evil was biological and endemic among all Jews. Ironically, this racist doctrine again resurfaced in Europe 430 years later in Nazi Germany and was used as the cornerstone for its political and racial theories for the Final Solution.

Many of the New Christians fled to northern Portugal, where they sought safety in the mountains, emigrating to cities and villages such as Carzão, Belmonte, Fundão and Moncorvo. The church was still not satisfied with the results and decided to officially reauthorize the Inquisition. For the next two centuries, the confiscation of all property, imprisonment, torture and death in the flames of the "auto-da-fe" (the act of faith) caused 40,000 Jews to suffer. The last death of a secret Jew occurred in Lisbon in 1755. Only recently have those who chose to risk their lives by staying in Portugal openly returned to Judaism. Thousands of Portuguese and Spanish Jews left the Iberian peninsula in the late fourteenth through eighteenth centuries. A new diaspora was eventually formed with large and influential Jewish communities arising in Goa, India, Amsterdam, London, Thessaloniki, Istanbul, Sarajevo and Rhodes. Eventually, they would spread to the Americas, first in Brazil, then in New Amsterdam (New York).

Officially, the Inquisition was abolished on March 31, 1821, but few Jews returned to Portugal. Not until 1868 were Jews permitted to buy land and construct a cemetery. Then, during the latter part of the nineteenth century, Jews from Gibraltar and Morocco established communities in Lisbon and Faro. Finally, after the establishment of the republic of Portugal in 1910, the government officially approved the re-establishment of the Jewish community. This meant the rebuilding of the infrastructure: synagogues, Jewish schools, khevra kadisha, koshering facilities, etc., like any other European Jewish community.

Prior to World War II, Portugal contained approximately four hundred Portuguese Jews, with another 650 Jewish refugees who had fled from Central Europe. Although Portugal was officially neutral during the war, President Salazar's close friendship with Franco and Hitler—and the continued pressure from the Catholic Church—resulted in making life difficult. Upon approval from Salazar, a political reactionary church organization "Accão Catolica" (Catholic Action) was formed. "Accão Catolica" created hysteria among the Christian Portuguese by implying that the refugees (mainly Jews) would cause widespread unemployment and that many of them were communist agents working for the Russians. This anti-Semitic propaganda resulted in Jewish-owned shops being boycotted, Jews being shunned and slandered and the Yeshivah in Oporto being closed.

When France fell to the Germans, Salazar was pressured by many close Jewish associates to adopt a more liberal policy towards Jewish immigrants. Again concerned about communist infiltration, Salazar's policy continued to exclude Jews of Russian origin. During the second half of the war, Portugal granted visas only to those Jews who were transiting through the country. During this time, Portuguese diplomat Aristides De Sousa Mendes, working out of the Portuguese embassy in Paris, helped save thousands of Jews, particularly those in Hungary, by granting them consular protection in the German-occupied lands. After the war, the Jewish community increased to 3,000, but most left for Israel or the United States.

Today, there are 600 Jews in the country, about half are Sephardim and half Ashkenazim.

Another 2,000 Conversos (hidden Jews) still live primarily north of Lisbon in the mountains and rural towns. They still practice many Jewish rites, such as lighting Shabbat candles on Friday evening and refraining from bread during Passover, with great sincerity and feeling for traditions. Although these hidden Jews could become part of the recognized Jewish community, the powerful psychological effect of having hidden their Judaism for five centuries has caused them to feel comfortable practicing Catholicism outside the home and Judaism inside the home. Rarely do they marry outside of their own clan and rarely do they speak with foreigners, particularly curious journalists. Ironically, they are known as Judeo (Port: Jews) by their gentile neighbors, but world Jewry does not recognize them as Jews.

The recognized Portuguese Jewish community today is small, with little communal infrastructure, and is gradually disappearing due to death, assimilation and emigration to Israel. Five hundred years after its origin, the Jewish community of Portugal is barely a remnant of its former grand self. Most likely, it will not celebrate another half millennium of existence.

# LISBON

*J*ews were already settled in Lisbon prior to the thirteenth century, when the country was under Moorish control. After the first Christian king, Alfonso I (1139–85), was crowned, the Jews remained in relative peace for two centuries. In 1260 King Alfonso III (1248–79) appointed a chief rabbi to be responsible for all the Jews in Portugal. His residence and official Jewish court was in Lisbon.

Throughout the fourteenth and early part of the fifteenth century, Jewish life prospered in Lisbon, despite occasional anti-Semitic outbreaks from the general public. Some of the most noteworthy Jews in Lisbon at this time were members of the Ibn Yahya family of scholars and financiers and the Toledano family of printers.

After the expulsion of the Jews from Spain in 1492, nearly 150,000 sought refuge in Portugal. Many came to Lisbon, and the Judiaria (Jewish quarters) soon became oppressively crowded, leading to an outbreak of the plague. Immediately, the city council ordered the Jews to leave their quarters and reside outside the city walls.

At the end of 1496, the expulsion and Inquisition of the Jews became official. Like all the other communities in Portugal, the Jewish community in Lisbon was forced to embrace Christianity or be expelled. Many chose to leave, eventually settling and creating new "Portuguese" Jewish communities in such cities as Izmir and Thessaloniki. Others converted, and sincerely embraced, Catholicism. Many who went to the baptismal font became New Christians (conversos), but clandestinely kept their Jewish faith. During the next 250 years, the "hidden Jews" and the New Christians, who willingly accepted Christianity, were repeatedly subjected to violent acts. Often, the beatings culminated with the auto-da-fe (burning at the pyre), which took place in the Rossio Plaza, the main market square

in Lisbon. This tribunal lasted from 1540 to 1755, castigating and subjecting even Jews and their offspring who had fled. Portuguese and Spanish Jews were forcibly taken back to their country from as far away as Central and South America for a trial and death by the auto-da-fe.

In 1755, a huge earthquake destroyed nearly all of Lisbon. The earthquake also triggered a devastating fire and tidal wave which completed the destruction of the city, including most of the Judiaria. Ironically, this natural disaster brought an end to the tribunal. Many of the lay people and priests believed the earthquake was a divine signal from heaven ordering the end of the torturous murders and the rebuilding of Lisbon.

Beginning in the nineteenth century, Jews began to return to the city in small numbers, re-establishing a community in 1813. The majority came from Gibraltar (British citizens) and a few from North Africa. Their numbers slowly increased until they numbered about 1,000 at the turn of the century. In 1902, the cornerstone of the first synagogue to be built in Portugal since before the decree of expulsion was laid on the street Rua Alexandre Herculano 59. The synagogue Shaare Tikva was completed in 1912. A beautiful, large, Moorish-style structure, the synagogue stood in the center of a courtyard surrounded by an iron fence and gate. Synagogues were not allowed to have their entrances directly at the foot of the street and no signs on the external wall facing the street could indicate that it was a synagogue. It was not until 1928, in Oporto, that the first synagogue was built with its entrance directly open to the street.

During World War II, Lisbon became the processing center for some 45,000 Jewish refugees fleeing German-occupied Europe. Most did not remain, but proceeded onward to homes in other countries. A large number traveled to South America.

After the war, some 3,000 Jews remained in Lisbon. Over the years, the community decreased in size until, today, it numbers about 350 or 400. This abatement is due to emigration to Israel (particularly during the Angola war) and assimilation due to intermarriage. From 1954 to 1970 Portugal was at war with the Angolan nationalist underground army, desperately trying to keep their colony from gaining independence. Most of the Jewish youth opposed Salazar's African war and left for Israel in the 1960s. There has been no formal Hebrew school in Lisbon since 1940 because of the noticable gap in the generation of Jewish youth between the ages of ten and thirty and living in Lisbon.

Today, Rabbi Abraham Assor, the only rabbi in Lisbon (there is one other in the country, Rabbi Sebag of Belmonte), instructs an occasional boy studying for his Bar Mitzvah. Most of the cultural and secular activities, involving some twenty children, meet at the Jewish Community Center and are organized by a few parents. The synagogue is the center for all formal religious activities. Unfortunately, being able to maintain a feeling of community is one of the main problems facing this tiny community. Dissension has split the small active community members into two factions. One group is led by a man who formed his own separate minyan which meets in an apartment on most Shabbats. He is currently the president of the Jewish Center. Those who

are opposed to his ideas on how to maintain a Jewish community do not frequent it. They feel the Jewish Center has become more like a private club and have decided to organize activities on their own. I attended one such Tu B'shvat outing.

Because of this dissension, the future of the community might lie—oddly enough—in the hands of the Jewish immigrants who, in the last ten years, have been moving to communities near Lisbon—"on the line" as it is euphemistically known. These "new" immigrants live in resort communities located near the sea just south of Lisbon. To go there, one takes a short train ride "on the line" that stops at the resort communities. One such place is Cascais, where many wealthy young and active retired emigres from South Africa, England, the United States and Israel come to enjoy sunny, inexpensive Portugal. They bring with them a strong sense of Jewish identity and involvement resulting in the formation of Hebrew classes, lectures on various Jewish topics, field trips, communal holiday celebrations (Passover, Chanukah) and successful fund raising campaigns for domestic and international Jewish causes.

The Jews in Lisbon will struggle to have a viable community for another generation into the twenty-first century. But the community "on the line" will continue to grow, and probably become a mirror image of those Jewish communities on the Costa del Sur.

Lisbon: The Jewish Community Center.

Lisbon: Sha'arey Tikvah synagogue, built in 1912.

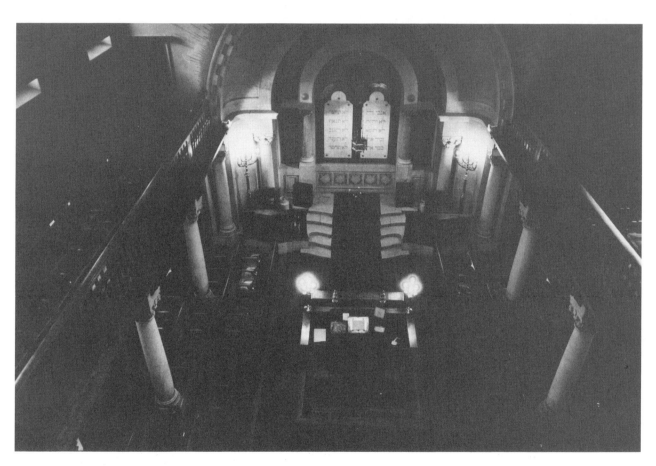

Lisbon: The view from the women's gallery in the Sha'arey Tikvah synagogue.

לוח אזכרה
לנשמות הנשמות ע"ח

À MEMÓRIA DE

DAVID ZAGURY
FORTUNATO ABECASSIS
ISAAC E HELENA ABECASSIS
JACOB HALPERN
JACOB JOSÉ LEVY
D. JOAQUIM BENSAUDE
JOSÉ E RACHEL BENSAUDE
LEÃO E ESTELLA AMZALAK
MARCOS E LEAH ZAGURY
MIRCEA SAIN
MOSES E THEA SEQUERRA
RAPHAEL BENOLIEL
SALOMÃO E SOFIA SAIN

E DOS DEPORTADOS, PELOS NAZIS, DE FRANÇA

ALBERTO SAMUEL TIANO
SARA E BELINA CUERON

Lisbon: A plaque inside the synagogue lists Portuguese
Jews living in France who were deported by the Nazis
to the concentration camps.

Lisbon: This corner building on Rua Monte De Olivete
16, was the place where Jewish refugees from throughout
Europe were processed before they went to their final
destination.

Lisbon: The various charities for the support of the
Jewish community to which Jews are encouraged to
donate when leaving the synagogue.

Lisbon: At "Sheloshim" services for Joseph
Ruah's (r.) mother, his youngest son, David,
stands to his left. Rabbi Abraham Assor leads
the solemn service.

Lisbon: Joshua Ruah washes his hands after visiting the Jewish cemetery.
The Hebrew translation: *"Our hands did not cause this death."*

Lisbon: Two Jewish cemeteries remain in Lisbon today. This one, begun in 1876, is still in use. The other is closed.

Lisbon: Until 1988 the kosher butcher shop, today it is used only occasionally.

Lisbon: The former Judiaria.

Lisbon: Jewish children on a Tu' B'Shvat outing in a part near Sesimbra.

Lisbon: Ralphy Bensadon (r.), originally from Madrid, and Henrique Ettner are the leaders of the Jewish youth group.

Lisbon: Children from the Jewish Community Center playing soccer.

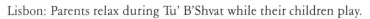

Lisbon: Parents relax during Tu' B'Shvat while their children play.

Lisbon: A young Portuguese Jewish girl.

Lisbon: Celebrating the planting of a tree on Tu' B'Shvat.

Lisbon: Chief Rabbi Abraham Assor, shown studying in his home, originally came from Tangier and has been Lisbon's rabbi, mohel and shokhet since 1945.

Lisbon: The Rossio Plaza in the heart of old Lisbon, where hundreds of Jews were tried and burned at the stake during the Inquisitions.

# Spain

The first Jewish settlers in Spain are believed to have been exiled to the Iberian peninsula after the First Temple in Jerusalem was destroyed in 586 B.C.E. Some scholars claim that the Jews and Phoenicians established towns with Hebrew sounding names, such as Malaga (Hebrew malacha-work), Toledo (Hebrew toledot-generations) and Sevilla (Hebrew shefelah-the plain).

After the fall of the Roman Empire, the Jews came under the rule of the Germanic Visigoths who governed from their court in Toledo in 421 B.C.E. For nearly two generations, the Jews lived in relative peace, until, in 587 B.C.E., King Reccared converted from Arianism to Catholicism. For the next 124 years the Jews were repeatedly persecuted. They were told only Catholics could reside in Spain, were forcibly baptized, had to sell all their slaves, buildings, land and vineyards at fixed low prices and were physically beaten. Finally, under the edict of King Egica (686–701), the Jews were reduced to slavery. During these years some Jews escaped and settled in North Africa. Those who stayed became the first community of New Christians (conversos).

In 711, with the invasion of the Arab Muslims across the straits of Gibraltar from North Africa, the Jews' suffering at the hands of the Visigoth kings came to an end. When the Arabs captured Córdoba, Granada, Sevilla and Toledo, the Jews readily helped their new rulers defeat the Visigoths. Under Muslim rule, the Jews immediately found new vocations as city life once again became important in Spain. Muslims depended heavily upon the Jews for their international commerce connections and sagacity for financial and state administration matters.

Jewish scholarship began to flourish during this time with the Babylonian Talmudic scholars corresponding with their counterparts in the cities of Lucena and Barcelona. Not until the reign of Caliph Abd-al Rahman III (912–971) in Córdoba, however, did the renaissance of Sephardic culture really begin to blossom. One of the leaders of this remarkable revival was Hasdai ibn Shaprut (915–970), who was personally employed by the Caliph as his chief physician and diplomat. Hasdai's patronage of Jewish culture, particularly of the poets Menachem ben Saruk and Dunashben Labrat, endured. At this time, the Jewish literati raised the level of their own Hebrew language to the high aesthetic level achieved by Arabic poetry and the famous "Golden Age" of Spain (from the 10th to 12th centuries) began for Hebrew literature, poetry and Rabbinic studies. As a result of this scholarly renaissance, Spanish Jewry began to rely less and less on the Rabbinical commentaries coming from Babylonia. In the tenth century Spain had become the center of Jewish learning in the western world. Its noted scholars and poets included Solomon ibn-Gabriol, Judah Ha-Levi, Moses ibn-Ezra, Asher ibn-Yechiel and Moses ben-Nachman (Nachmanides).

Relatively tolerant rulers encouraged Jewish financiers, writers, scholars and scientists and a Jewish upper class was created. One of the most remarkable Jewish personalities coming from this echelon was Samuel ibn-Nagrella, commonly known as Samuel ha-Nagid. Fluent in Arabic, Hebrew and Spanish, Samuel ha-Nagid, a refugee from Córdoba, served as vizier of the Kingdom of Badis and commander of the army of Granada. A writer of poetry and commentaries from the Torah and Talmud, he appointed his son Joseph to succeed him as though in a dynastic succession. It soon became evident to the Muslim rulers that the real power in the kingdom was in the hands of a Jew. Resentment culminated in the killing of Joseph ha-Nagid and an attack upon the Jews of Granada. The Granada massacre, in 1066, resulted in some 3,000 Jewish deaths and would be the watershed in the beginning of sporadic anti-Jewish outbursts from the ruling Muslims.

During the Muslim rule, the Sephardic community garnered its distinct characteristics which made it quite different from the Ashkenazic pietists of the day. In the poetry of the Jewish courtiers—those who served as models for the general Jewish populace—we read about men who enjoyed the pleasures of life. Loving literature and science, as well as the traditional observances, they cultivated ambition and wealth as well as erotic passion. From that time on, wherever the Sephardim settled, they carried their sense of pedigree as a cloak of distinction and were purveyors of high culture.

At the beginning of the eleventh century, the Christian kingdoms of the north slowly began to reconquer the Muslim kingdoms of the south. The Muslims were routed, but the Jews were encouraged to stay and help rebuild the cities. The Christian rulers took full advantage of the Jews' scientific knowledge, commercial contacts, finances, multi-lingual abilities and prowess in aesthetics. By the thirteenth century, Toledo was the largest Jewish community in Spain, with a population of 13,000.

A typical Jewish quarter (Spanish-call), was at that time a crowded, boisterous neighborhood, with a synagogue, mikveh (ritual bath), butcher shop, shoemaker, furrier, ceramicist and other small shops, a Talmud Torah and a bikur kholim (hospital), while a cemetery was outside the city walls. Supervising the internal affairs of the community were the members of the aljama (Spanish: Jewish ghetto), which generally consisted of members of the wealthiest families. They governed by their own ordinances, which were always subject to royal approval. They also imposed taxes on kosher meat and wine, Shabbat candles, weddings and visiting Jews. Revenue from these taxes was used to support the rabbi, shamash, gabbai, orphans, widows and the poor.

During this period, several social and religious conflicts were taking place in the aljamas that would have far reaching effects. The first controversy was over the writings of Rabbi Moses ben Maimon (also known as Maimonides or the Rambam), especially his epic work *Guide for the Perplexed,* which attempted to reconcile religion and philosophy. Consequently, many Jews who had been greatly influenced by Arab culture drew the conclusion from his work that one had to have a rational faith and properly understood beliefs; while the observance of the minutiae traditional precepts were no more than ornamentation and did not effect one's quest for eternal salvation. Disagreeing with this philosophy were the humble rabbis in France and Germany to the north. Under the guidance of the Tossafists (disciples of Rashi), they believed strict observance was the most efficacious way of preserving the Jewish identity in the diaspora and prevented any kind of assimilation that invariably led to extinction. The rabbis were so adamant about their beliefs that they declared a herem (anathema) against any Jew who, before the age of twenty five, studied philosophy or any other kind of non-religious sciences, except for Maimonides' works on medicine and astronomy.

The second major controversy came about from the re-emergence of Kabbalism, a movement that combined the philosophies of ancient Jewish mysticism and the pietism of the medieval German Jews. The movement spread widely through the writings of Nachmanides (Talmudic scholar and rabbi) and the Zohar, the veritable canon of Kabbala attributed to the Spanish Rabbi Moses Shem-Tov de Leon (1230–1305). The Zohar (book of splendor) authorship was spuriously attributed to the Rabbinic Sage of Judea Simeon bar Yochai in order to lend it greater authority.

The kabbalists found fault with aristocratic Sephardic society. They saw that the aristocrats and courtiers were often driven by the pursuit of pleasure, profit and political ambition, openly practicing polygamy while living an ostentatious way of life. On the other hand, the kabbalists practiced a completely opposite way of life. They lived a life of asceticism, kept a constant adherence to the Torah and preached monogamy and the advantages of rural life. In the midst of all these rivalries, the attitude of the Catholic monarchy vacillated from benevolent guardian to indifference. Finally, the sense of security the

aljamas enjoyed was shattered. In a riot against the Jews of Sevilla on June 4, 1391, scores of Jews were killed, many more forcibly baptized and many synagogues were burnt or converted into churches. Led by the virulent anti-Semitic preaching of the archdeacon of Ecija, the head of the diocese of Seville Ferrando Martinez fanned the flames of anti-Semitism, igniting more riots in Madrid, Aragon, Córdoba, Jaen, Toledo, Barcelona, the Balearic Islands and other sites.

The kings tried to rebuild the aljamas, but they were in complete disarray due to the problems of the sweeping forced and unforced conversions. Jewish families and friends ended up enemies because some had converted willingly and others forcibly. Others remained Jews. To compound the problems, the new converts continued living in the Jewish quarters. Soon, the authorities began enforcing the rules of the church. Nobody was to be converted against his will, but any person who had been baptized for whatever reason could not return to Judaism.

As was to be expected, Jews did everything they could to bring their family and friends back into the fold; while the converts who wished to remain Catholic tried every means to encourage their friends and families to be baptized. Unfortunately, these converts were filled with such a religious zeal that they persecuted Jews by becoming informants for the church, identifying those who practiced Judaism in secret and were known as the "hidden" or Marrano Jews. Compounding the problem, many rabbis lacked the moral fortitude necessary to confront the ordeal and act as leaders. Many rabbis hastened to the baptismal font and zealously reproached their brethren. Menahem ben Zerah changed his name to Juan Sanchez de Sevilla and became major of Sevilla. Solomon ha-Levi became Pablo de Santa Maria, the bishop of Burgos.

Soon, "New Christian" courtiers replaced the Jewish courtiers in all phases of social standing and government. Most Jews were now craftsmen, small traders or shopkeepers. Most doctors were still Jewish. Before long, the old Christians became resentful that the converts were taking the most lucrative posts and using their influence to economically enhance their businesses. The church found that many of these converts (Spanish-conversos) were secretly practicing Judaism. Immediately, the church deemed that the focal problem for all the country's civil strife was due to the close proximity in which the Jews and converts lived. As long as they lived together it would be impossible to make the New Christians faithful Catholics. Consequently, in 1480, Jews were forced to live in new districts on the outskirts of the cities, the intention being to separate them from the rest of society.

The first Inquisition began in 1481 in Sevilla. During the next ten years, the Catholic church used every conceivable weapon—including death by burning at the stake—to kill some 13,000 New Christians, who, in actuality, were hidden Jews—the worst kind of heretics according to the Church. Most of the executions were done in huge plazas, where the Christian public could come and witness the spectacle. New converts who were present would become terrified and worry if they were next.

The last Muslim bastion fell on January 2, 1492. In the Alhambra in Granada, on March 31, 1492, King Ferdinand and Queen Isabella signed the edict expelling the Jews from Spain. All those Jews who would not convert would have to leave. In May the exodus began. Jews had to liquidate all property as quickly and as best they could. Many sold their homes, vineyards, shops and personal belongings just for a donkey. On July 31, two days before Tisha B-Av, the last Jews of Spain were officially expelled. Initially, some 150,000 Sephardic Jews sought refuge in Portugal, only to be expelled once again when the Portuguese Inquisition came into full force in 1496. These Jews and their descendants gradually spread to North Africa (mostly Morocco), other countries along the Mediterranean shores and throughout the Ottoman Empire. Later, in the seventeenth

and eighteenth centuries, large Sephardic communities were established in Paris, Amsterdam, Hamburg and London.

After 1492, no professing Jew lived in Spain until the latter part of the nineteenth century because the Inquisition did not officially end until 1834. In 1869, non-Catholics were granted the rights of freedom of religion and residence. During the last quarter of the nineteenth century, Jews from Morocco and Czarist Russia trickled back into Madrid and Sevilla. Then, in 1909, the law prohibiting the building of synagogues was rescinded. The Spanish government decreed, in 1924, that any person of Sephardic origin was entitled to Spanish citizenship. It was the intention of the government to attract Sephardim to Spain, particularly those from the former lands of the Ottoman Empire. Only a small number responded. From 1933 to the beginning of the Spanish Civil War, some 3,000 Jewish Central European refugees found a safe haven in Spain. During the Civil War (1936–37), most Jews left the country. All non-Catholic communities had to close. Of the few Jews who stayed, most fought against Franco and his nationalist army.

During World War II, the Jewish population increased due to the refugees fleeing occupied France. Most of these Jews stayed only briefly and continued on to Portugal. In the beginning of the war, General Franco, who was Hitler's close friend, either arrested and deported Jews fleeing from southern France back to Vichy France or detained them in the Miranda de Ebro concentration camp. When the tide of the war began to turn in favor of the Allies, the Spanish government became a bit more lenient. In 1943, the Spanish consulates in Europe were instructed to issue Spanish passports to any Jew of Sephardic origin, even those who were in concentration camps, and have them transported back to Spain. But the Final Solution had already been implemented. Eichmann pressured the Spanish government to allow only those Jews who could prove their Spanish citizenship to enter Spain.

Thousands of Sephardic Jews whose ancestors were from Spain, but could not prove Spanish citizenship, perished. At the end of the war, some 8,500 Jews survived in Spain, including 2,750 Hungarian Jews who were specifically saved during the Allied rescue operations in the spring of 1944.

In 1967, Spain finally issued a formal repeal of the edict of expulsion. The first new synagogue since the twelfth century was built in Madrid in 1968. This event was explicitly felt by all Jews and initiated the slow revival of Jewish life in Spain.

Today, there are about thirteen thousand Jews in Spain. Most are Sephardim from Morocco with a few from the Balkans, while the small Ashkenazic community is comprised of Jews from Central and Eastern Europe. In recent years the community has been growing, with new Jewish immigrants arriving from South America, lured to the country's growing economy and common language. This steady increase in the Jewish population has been responsible for the formation of twelve official communities located in Madrid, Barcelona, Valencia, Palm de Mallorca, Alicante, Málaga, Marbella, Sevilla, Ceuta and Mellila.

Assimilation and intermarriage are still problems, but not as serious as in other Sephardic communities I visited. Recent interest by Jews and non-Jews throughout the world, particularly in preserving Sephardic folk music and the language of Judeo-Spanish, gives Jewish life in Spain a promising future.

Sevilla: A passageway through the former Juderia, Barrio de Santa Cruz.

# MADRID

Madrid, the capital of Spain since 1561 and the reign of King Phillip II, was not a major Jewish center until the twentieth century. Only when the Jewish community was re-established in Madrid did the focus of Spanish Jewry turn toward the capital. Today, Madrid (5,000) and Barcelona (6,000) have the two most active communities in the country.

Although a small community existed during Muslim rule, Madrid's growth and activism came after it was captured by the Catholics in 1083. For the next three hundred years, the community managed to prosper despite numerous restrictions imposed by various kings at the urging of the church, including holding official positions and owning land.

A tremendous anti-Jewish hysteria swept the country in 1391, resulting in the massacre of thousands of Jews and the destruction and confiscation of their property. Most fled the city. Others remained and became "New Christians," while a few, despite extreme difficulties, maintained an open Jewish identity.

The church was determined to eradicate anyone and anything remotely connected to Judaism. In 1478, the local court ordered all Jews and Moors to wear a distinctive badge on their outer clothing. If they were observed not wearing the badge, they were severely punished. Fourteen years later, after the official decree of expulsion was signed by King Ferdinand and Queen Isabella, the Jewish community in Madrid ceased to formally exist.

When Madrid became the capital of Spain, the Supreme Tribunal made its home in the city. It brought with it the auto-da-fe and its horrible public displays. Several hundred "New Christians" and Moricos (Muslim converts to Christianity) were burned at the stake in the infamous plaza known today as Plaza de Major.

After its reestablishment early in the nineteenth century, the Jewish community grew slowly, with an influx of refugees from Nazi Germany in the 1930s, but suffered greatly again during the Spanish Civil War when most Jews openly supported the Loyalists against Franco's Nationalists.

The small community used an apartment on Pissaro Street as a synagogue and community center until the Inquisition and decree of expulsion were finally rescinded by the Spanish government in 1968. The first synagogue to be built since 1391 was opened on Calle Balmes 3 on that date.

Today, Beth Yaacov Synagogue is part of a large community center that houses an assembly hall, library, kosher kitchen, youth lounge, Beit Midrash and offices for the rabbi and staff.

Of the four rabbis in Madrid, three originally came from Morocco: Chief Rabbi Benasuly, Rabbi Bendahan and Rabbi Garzon. The Lubavitcher Rabbi Goldstein comes from New York. They all work with a community approximately ninety percent Moroccan, eight percent European and two percent South American. Most of the Moroccan Jews arrived in the past twenty years. Some lived in Spanish Mellila and Ceuta, while others resided in the Northern Morocco cities Tangiers, Casablanca and Larache. They carried Spanish identification cards and felt and spoke Spanish as their everyday language. Jews from further south in Agadir, Marrakech or Safi were more Berber-like, spoke French and immigrated primarily to France instead of Spain.

The Madrid community is proud of its Jewish Day School, Colegio Estrella Toledano, located in the affluent suburb of Moralija. Begun in 1965, the school was originally established with only twelve students in a small apartment. The present school was built in 1977 and has 215 students, some Israelis and others non-Jewish. Forty non-Jewish students attend because the school has a reputation for high scholarship, a friendly milieu and offers classes in English, French, Hebrew and Spanish.

My research in Madrid was interrupted by the Gulf War. Security in the Jewish community was tightened considerably and the community elders were understandably disconcerted. Just as I was becoming discouraged at the thought that I might not be able to accomplish any work, the warm welcome I received from the principal, her staff and the pupils at the school made my stay in Madrid worthwhile and memorable.

# TOLEDO

Toledo was the capital of Spain until 1561.

Jews more than likely established a settlement a thousand years before Toledo became the capital of the Visigoth Kingdom. When the Visigoths converted to Christianity in 587, they immediately began harassing Jews, and, by 613, the Jews were forced to choose between baptism or expulsion from the kingdom. For over a hundred years, thousands either converted, left Spain or, depending on the tolerant or intolerant attitudes of succeeding Visigoth rulers, remained and attempted to survive.

In 711, the Muslims crossed the straits of Gibraltar into Spain, destroying the Christian kingdom, and, for over four hundred years, the Jewish community prospered under their Muslim rulers. During this time, the Juderia (Jewish quarter), which existed until the expulsion of the Jews in 1492, was built.

During the eleventh and twelfth centuries, Toledo was one of the leading European centers of scholarship, attracting Jews from Spain, North Africa and Western Europe. The Jewish population reached 12,000 in the middle of the twelfth century. With its many synagogues, yeshivot, writers, poets, doctors, historians and Hebrew grammarians—all amassed behind a fortress wall high above the Tajus River—Toledo became known as the "Jerusalem of Spain."

Toledo's School of Translators was world renowned. Jewish, Muslim and Christian scholars translated works of mathematics, astronomy, medicine, religious texts and other subjects from Arabic and Hebrew into Latin to be disseminated and used throughout Europe. Scholars of medieval European history have attributed it to being one of the catalytic institutions that initiated the Renaissance in Europe.

Many Jewish scholars and writers lived and worked in Toledo during this time. Among them were: Meir ibn Megas (1077–1141), who established an academy for the study of the Talmud; Abraham ibn Daud (c.1110–80), a historian who concentrated extensively on Spanish Jewish history; Abraham ibn Ezra (1092–1167), a grammarian and interpreter of the Bible whose commentaries still accompany the text of most Hebrew editions; and Judah Ha-Levi (c.1086–1145), probably the most noted Jewish literary figure associated with the "Golden Age of Spain," a physician philosopher and one of the greatest Hebrew poets.

More than in any other Spanish city today, one can still see in Toledo remnants of a once-glorious Jewish community. Two such synagogues, the Santa Maria la Blanca and the El Tránsito, still stand. The Santa Maria la Blanca originally is believed to have been built in the early thirteenth century by Joseph Abu Omar ibn Shoshan, a friend of Alfonso III. Standing in a quiet garden in the heart of the former Juderia, it seems outwardly unimpressive, but inside it is ornately decorated with Moorish and Jewish motifs. Converted to a church in 1405, it later became a military barracks, a warehouse and a dancehall. Today, it is a museum.

Down the street, the more famous El Tránsito was built in 1357 with funds from Samuel ben Meir Halevi Abulafia, a treasurer and close advisor to King Don Pedro. Erected by Rabbi Meyer Abdeli, the most renowned architect of the period, assisted by Moorish craftsmen, it was patterned after the magnificent Alhambra in his native Granada. Ironically, Abulafia did not see its completion. He was accused of disloyalty and subjected to a torturous death by the rack in Sevilla. In 1492, the Inquisition transformed the synagogue into the Church of Notre

Dame—thus the name "Tránsito" (transition). In 1550 the building became an asylum, then a military barracks in 1798. Finally, it was recognized as a national monument at the end of the nineteenth century. Today, it, too, is a museum, located directly across the street from the palatial home of Abulafia. In 1585, the gifted painter El Greco moved into part of the house around which legends and rumors of Abulafia's treasure hidden in the catacombs persisted for years.

The grandeur of Jewish life in medieval Toledo began to disintegrate at the beginning of the fourteenth century. Civil wars, persecutions from the church, riots, the Black Plague epidemic and fires brought ruin and destruction. Finally, in 1492, the Jews of Toledo accompanied the rest of the country's Jews into exile. Their synagogues, homes, businesses and fields were confiscated by the crown. A small number of conversos (hidden Jews) continued to live in the city through the 1660s, but eventually fell victim to the auto-da-fe. Only a few managed to escape to Morocco.

Considering the prosperity and degree of scholarship, it is sad to comprehend what befell the Jews of Toledo. Many rabbis and lay Jews believe the herem (act of banishment) should still be honored, not because the Jews cannot return and settle, but because the city is not deserving enough for the reestablishment of a Jewish community.

As a result, Toledo is virtually void of any Jewish life today. Thousands traverse the streets of the former Juderia every year, but only as tourists, gazing and wondering about the Jewish splendors of the past.

Toledo: Next to the El Tránsito synagogue stands the palatial villa of Samuel Abulafia, which houses the El Greco Museum.

# SEVILLA

*L*egend has it that Jews first settled in Sevilla after the destruction of the First Temple in 586 B.C.E. Some of the most famous families—among them the Abrabanels—claim descent from King David. We know that there was a Jewish settlement during the reign of the Visigoths and, when the Muslims conquered the city in 712, the Jews remained under the new rulers.

Sevilla prospered under the Muslims and became an important cultural center. Jews were involved in commerce, medicine and virtually controlled the dying industry.

In the eleventh century, Sevilla had an influx of Jews from several different areas. They came from Córdoba fleeing the Berber conquest, from Granada fleeing the anti-Jewish riots and from North Africa seeking economic improvement.

Some prominent Jews lived in Sevilla during the Golden Age: Isaac ben Baruch Albalia, head of the Jewish community and court astrologer; Abraham ben Meir, who later became head of the community and vizier to the king; and the poets Abu Sulayman ibn Mujahir and Abul al-Fath Elezar ibn Azhar.

Following the reconquest of Sevilla by the Christians in 1248, the Jewish community continued to prosper and build new synagogues, reaching a total of twenty three by the beginning of the fourteenth century. As the city's port extended trade to other ports in Spain, Portugal and North Africa, the Jewish community's contacts with other Jewish communities increased.

During the twelfth and mid-thirteenth centuries, the Jews were still subjected to an inordinate amount of taxes and restrictions, but, overall, enjoyed a relatively tranquil existence. This tranquility ended in 1378 when the young archdeacon of Ecija, Ferrant Martinez, encouraged the public to riot against the Jewish community. Many Jews were killed as properties and synagogues were confiscated. Then, in 1390, the Jews found a friend in King Henry III, who ordered the archbishop to restore all properties and synagogues. Later he publicly castigated the fanatical clergyman.

This reprieve lasted only a year. Spain's anti-Jewish sentiments again swept across the country in full fury, destroying and killing everything and anything Jewish. Synagogues were turned into churches, workshops and homes, and land was confiscated. Hundreds were murdered. At this time, the Jewish population had reached some 20,000.

Over the next hundred years the community rapidly declined, soon consisting only of a small group of Jews and a larger number of conversos. Before the official decree of expulsion from Spain in March, 1492, some seven hundred Jews were burned at the stake, while another five thousand were forcibly baptized. In 1492, Sevilla was one of the main ports of embarkation for thousands of exiles, most of whom initially traveled to North Africa. At the port, the inquisitors investigated and searched every departing ship, looking for conversos. Incredibly, this practice lasted into the early part of the nineteenth century, when the Inquisition was finally officially abolished.

The first Jews to return came in 1881—as indicated by graves found in the Jewish cemetery. They were mostly from North Africa and Gibraltar. In the 1920s thirty or forty families comprised the community, joined later in the 1930s by refugees fleeing from Nazi Germany.

Presently, sixty to seventy Jews live in Sevilla, of which there are only four or five families where both spouses are Jewish. Many of the Jews in Sevilla come from Ceuta and Mellila,

Spanish ruled Moroccan cities.

For the last sixteenth years an apartment owned by a Jewish woman who lived in Ceuta had served as the community's synagogue, which had two Sepher Torahs, one from Ceuta belonging to the president of the community, Mr. Simon Hassan Benasayag, and the other from Madrid. Getting a minyan for Shabbat, or even for the High Holidays, is very difficult. When there is a minyan for prayer services, it often consists of Israeli and/or American students and tourists. Recently, the woman from Ceuta returned to Sevilla and reclaimed her apartment. Currently, the community is searching for a new apartment to serve as the synagogue.

One evening, I met Mr. Hassan Benasayag, his wife and oldest child, Deborah, at the pub bar, Solomon-El Rey de los Pinchitos, owned by their good Jewish friend Abraham Benhanu Balilty, who was originally from Mellila. We enjoyed a snack of beer, olives and bread, while we discussed the future of Sevilla's Jewish community. Deborah had just returned to Spain after having lived for eleven years in Israel. She plans to begin teaching Hebrew to some of the children and adults in the community, including Abraham's two young daughters. Hassan told me that, though the future looked bleak, he felt Sevilla's Jewish community would last at least another generation or two: "There are some Jews moving from Madrid who want to live in a smaller and more beautiful city, while perhaps some of the Jews from South America who are immigrating to Spain will choose to live here."

After our snack and conversation, I bid goodbye to my new friends and, in the cool starry night, walked back to my pension located in the former Juderia known as Barrio de Santa Cruz. Walking through the narrow cobblestone streets of the old city, one could hear the sounds of laughter, music and clinking glasses emanating from the crowded pubs. I could only imagine what sounds must have emanated through the Juderia seven hundred years before.

# CÓRDOBA

Some historians speculate that Jews living in Córdoba helped the Muslims conquer the city in 711. Actual written sources mention a Jewish settlement in 840. During the reign of the caliph Abd-el Rahman III (912–61) Córdoba became a Jewish and Muslim cultural center. The caliph had invited Arab philosophers, poets and scientists to settle in Córdoba. Following his example, Hasdai ibn Shaprut (c. 925–75), personal physician and diplomat to the caliph, invited many brilliant Jewish philosophers, poets and rabbinical scholars. Ibn Shaprut's home became a gathering place for poets to read their latest works and rabbis to discuss their latest commentaries. Among these academic luminaries were Rabbi Moses ben Hanokh, who was brought from Italy and was responsible for the revival of Talmudic studies in Spain, and Rabbi Menachem ben Saruk, who compiled a comprehensive Hebrew dictionary and grammar book. Among the poets the most famous was Judah Ha-Levi (1075–1141), who, though born in Toledo, lived most of his life in Córdoba. Ha-Levi's verses are considered the greatest examples of medieval Hebrew poetry and have found their way into Jewish liturgy.

The most famous Jewish personality born in Córdoba did not remain. Moses ben Maimon, or Moses Maimonides, was born in Córdoba in 1135. At the age of thirteen, he and his family fled the city when the Almohades, fanatical Berber tribesmen from North Africa, crossed the straits of Gibraltar, conquering all of Andalusia, including Córdoba. Following the conquest, much of the Jewish quarter was destroyed and the Jews were forced to adopt Islam. Though Maimonides' theological, philosophical and medical career was spent in Palestine and Egypt, the Jews of Spain—then and now—are proud to claim him as a native son.

Down the street from where Maimonides was born, on 20 Calle do los Judios, stands the only synagogue in the city today. Built in 1315 by Issac Moheb ben Ephraim, the synagogue and adjoining room were used for the community's small beit din (house of law), as well as prayers. At the end of the fifteenth century, when the Jews were expelled from Córdoba, the synagogue was converted into the Church of St. Crispan.

In 1884, two Christian scholars called public attention to the building as a former synagogue and the Spanish government restored it and declared it a national monument. In 1935, during the celebration of the octocentennial of Maimonides' birth, Jewish delegates from all over the world held Hebrew prayers in the synagogue for the first time in 443 years.

Soon after the Christian conquest in 1235 anti-Jewish restrictions, including heavy taxation, were introduced in Córdoba. Though smaller than Toledo, the community was still important to the crown's coffers.

In 1391, anti-Jewish riots killed most of the Jewish community in Córdoba, as well as the rest of Spain. When it became the headquarters for King Ferdinand and Queen Isabella during the war between the Christians and the Muslims, anti-Jewish measures were issued. Jews were ordered to leave Andalusia and finally expelled from all over the country in 1492.

As in most cities, a few Jews remained behind and lived as "hidden Jews," sometimes known as conversos. These conversos had a reputation as being so strongly attached to Judaism, despite the violent attacks, that it gave sufficient evidence to rabbinical courts throughout Europe to recognize them as Jews. The Inquisition in Córdoba was particularly cruel and remained active until the eighteenth century.

Today, only two Jews are known to live in Córdoba, hardly enough to support any kind of Jewish life. When one walks the narrow, picturesque streets of the former Juderia, one can only imagine the rich and vibrant Jewish life which once existed here.

Sevilla: Simon Hassan Benasayag, president of the Jewish community, with his wife and daughter at the pub Bar Solomon.

Toledo: The Santa Maria la Blanca, originally known as the Great Synagogue, was built sometime in the 13th century. Converted into a church in 1405, the interior is a forest of 32 pillars, supporting a long vista of octagonal arches.

Toledo: The El Tránsito synagogue, built by Samuel ben-Meier Halevi Abulafia in 1357, received its name when the Inquisition transformed it into a Benedictine monastery, hence *"Tránsito"* (Transition).

Toledo: The interior of the El Tránsito synagogue. It's carved ceiling, made of cedar and inlaid with mother-of-pearl, stands forty feet above the tiled sanctuary floor. The four walls are covered with filigree-like stone with verses from the Psalms, also carved into stone.

Cordoba: The women's gallery in the Rambam synagogue, located near the Rambam's birthplace.

Sevilla: Formerly a synagogue, the Church of Santa Maria la Blanca was a gift from King Alfonso the Wise to the Jews of Sevilla.

Sevilla: The third floor apartment on Calle Peral 10, formerly the synagogue for the small Jewish community.

Madrid: A recent Jewish emigre from Chile studies in the Beit Midrash.

Madrid: Rabbi Garson (l.) talking with the Lubavitcher Rabbi Goldstein, who has lived in Madrid since 1978.

Sevilla: Pub Bar Solomon.

Madrid: The only kosher butcher shop in the city. The owners are originally from Tangier, Morocco.

Madrid: The khevra kadishe (Heb. burial society) performing the "sheloshim" ceremony in the new Jewish cemetery in the town of Hoyo De Manzanares, 30 kilometers outside of Madrid.

Madrid: This small Jewish cemetery is now closed.

Toledo: A store selling Jewish antiques, located near the Santa Maria la Blanca synagogue.

Madrid: A view of the brit milah (Heb. circumcision) from the women's gallery in the Beth Yaacov synagogue.

Madrid: The nurse hands the baby to the sandek (Heb. godfather), while Chief Rabbi Benasuly looks on.

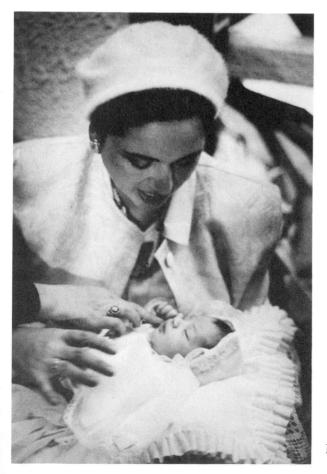

Madrid: Minutes before his brit milah, Rebbetzin Bendahan holds her baby boy.

Cordoba: A statue honoring Maimonides, erected by the Spanish government in 1964, stands in the Plazuela de Maimonides.

Cordoba: The carved plasterwork above the empty niche in the Rambam synagogue where the Holy Ark once stood.

Toledo:
Calle
Samuel
Levi in the
Juderia.

Toledo: A street sign in the former Jewish Quarter (Juderia).

Madrid: Lunch time for the elementary grades at the Day School. All meals are kosher.

Madrid: First graders learn English in the Jewish Day School.

Madrid: Riding the school bus to the Jewish Day School.

Sevilla: Abraham Benhamu Belilty, the owner of the popular pub Bar Solomon, is originally from Mellila.

Madrid: Jewish artists Adam (flamenco guitarist) and Laila (dancer), out for a walk with their twins.

Madrid: Dino Delmonte is a virtuoso tsimbalist, known for his beautiful Jewish and flamenco melodies.

Toledo: Sunrise over the "Jerusalem of Spain."

Madrid: In the heart of old Madrid is the Plaza Mayor, built by Philip III in 1619. Many were tried by the Inquisition and burned at the stake in this square.

Sevilla: A view of the Giralda Tower on the banks of the Guadalquivir River, from which thousands of Jews set sail for freedom during the expulsion. During the Inquisition, Jews also sought refuge in the tower from the city's marauding mobs.

# BIBLIOGRAPHY

Ausubel, Nathan. *Pictorial History of the Jewish People.* New York: Crown Publishers, Inc., 1954.

Comay, Joan. *The Diaspora Story: The Epic of the Jewish People Among the Nations.* New York: Random House, 1980.

Copsidas, Cotis. *Les Juifs De Thessalonique (1886–1917).* Thessaloniki, Greece, 1989.

Dawidowicz, Lucy S. *The War Against the Jews (1933–1945).* New York: Penguin USA, 1975.

*Encyclopedia of Judaica.* Jerusalem: Keter Publishing House, 1972.

Fernandez, Luis Suarez. *Judios Espanoles En La Edad Media.* Madrid: Ediciones Rialp, S.A., 1988.

Freedman, Warren. *The World Guide for the Jewish Traveler.* New York: E.P. Dutton, Inc., 1984.

Gilbert, Martin. *Atlas of Jewish History, Cartography by Arthur Banks.* New York: Dorset Press, 1984.

Hacohen, Rabbi Menachem and Dr. Dvora Hacohen. *One People: The Study of the Eastern Jews.* New York: Adama Books, 1986.

Lacave, J.L. and M. Ontanon Armengol. *Sefarad, Sefarad: La Espana Judia.* Madrid: Lunwerg Editores, S.A., 1987.

Lerman, Anthony. *The Jewish Communities of the World, 4th Edition.* New York: Institute of Jewish Affairs, Fact on File, Inc., 1989.

Patai, Raphael. *The Vanished Worlds of Jewry.* Picture Research by Eugene Rosow with Vivian Kleiman. New York: Macmillan Publishing Co., 1980.

Postal, Bernard and Samuel H. Abramson. *Traveler's Guide to Jewish Landmarks of Europe.* New York: Fleet Press Corp., 1971.

Strom, Yale. *A Tree Still Stands: Jewish Youth in Eastern Europe Today.* New York: Philomel Books, 1990.

Strom, Yale and Brian Blue. *The Last Jews of Eastern Europe.* New York: Philosophical Library, Inc., 1987.